Passing On
A Written Legacy

An Easy Guide to Memory Writing

by

Lana Rockwell

Cover Design and Layout by Chuck Haas Designs

Editing by Lee Horsman and Sonja Haas

Visit Lana at: mymemoriesforyou.net

The Memory Examples contained in this book are some of the stories my husband and I have written for our children and grandchildren. For this publication, I have changed the names of the people involved.

TABLE OF CONTENTS

This book is dedicated to my husband.
Without his encouragement, love, support
and prayers it might have been something
I only dreamed about
but never actually finished.

Do you like to tell stories?

Everyone has a story. I have yet to meet anyone who does not enjoy talking about their own life when they find someone who is genuinely interested in listening to what they have to say. From the moment of conception our stories begin. But what happens to those stories if they are left untold? I find it very sad that millions of people are living their lives without ever sharing their life experiences with their families or anyone else. What a tragedy! Future generations can learn so much from the experiences of others and they deserve to know their families' histories.

Do you enjoy the stories told or written by your parents or grandparents? As a small child I did not have the opportunity to hear the stories of my grandparents and, to my knowledge, they didn't record them anywhere. They were either deceased or quite elderly by the time I was old enough to want to hear their stories so, while my mother was still with us, I gleaned what I could from her. Because of the regret I carry of not hearing the stories of my grandparents, I decided to record my own memories for my children and grandchildren.

I don't know about your family, but my children/grandchildren don't gather around me as I sit in the rocking chair on the front porch, nor do they want to sit around the kitchen table listening to me tell stories of days-gone-by. Once in a while something will trigger a memory when we are together and I have the privilege of sharing a story, but those times are rare. They are watching their favorite sport on TV, playing a video or family game or listening to their iPod while our family history waits to be told or read.

"So," you might ask, "why do you want them to know your story?" I believe the more they know about where I came from, where I've been, what took me there, what happened while I was there, etc., the more they will understand who I am today and why I am who I am. Why don't I like chocolate covered cherries? Why do I have scars on my shoulder and on my face? Why do flowers and gardening give me so much joy? Why do I have a soft spot in my heart for couples who have lost a baby? I firmly believe my family has a right to know these things and, for the life of me, I don't ever see my children or my grandchildren sitting at my knee begging me to "tell them a story." With that in mind, I decided to put those stories in writing.

When people heard about "my project" they asked me to help them start doing the same thing for their families. I have often been asked "How do I get started?" or "Why don't you write a book teaching people how to write their memories?"

There is no doubt that many of you reading this book have been "blessed" with the same grandparent's "memory books" that I have. You know the ones...the "fill in the blank" type. Every time a precious little baby joined our family I got another pesky book to complete. I now have eight of them sitting on a shelf - not a single page has been filled out. I'm not saying there is anything wrong with those books. If the truth be known, they are certainly better than nothing. However, for me they are too generic or "cookie cutter." Yes, they give you a chance to record your favorite color, food, birthday, first kiss, etc. But they don't even scratch the surface of what I want my family to know about my story.

So, how do you get started? Well, let me ask you this... how do you lose weight? How do you finish reading a book? How did you get through school/college/vocational training, etc.? If you want a fresh, home baked chocolate cake for dinner tonight, what do you have to do? If you know the lawn needs to be mowed or the car needs to be washed, what do you have to do? To accomplish anything - be it large or small - you have to put one step in front of the other and get started, right? The same thing must happen with writing your memories and I am anxious for you to start writing - there is a deep sense of satisfaction from the moment you jot down your first memory. I believe you will never be sorry - and your family will be forever grateful. Does it seem like too big of a challenge? Let me address some things people have actually said to me as they wrestled with getting started that perhaps have you "stuck" and are keeping you from picking up that pen or sitting down in front of your computer:

"I Can't Remember Like You Do."

Once I started writing, many memories came flooding back - things that I had not thought about for years - and the same thing will happen to you. You never know when something is going to trigger a memory - it might be a scent or the smell of something, it might be a picture, it might be something someone says or something on TV. As soon as I get the chance, I add that memory to my list of topics to write about in the future. Keep pen and paper handy, not only by your computer, but in your purse or in your pocket, on the nightstand next to your bed, in the car, by the chair where you watch TV, etc. Listening to other people tell their stories helps with "memory recall." I have yet to be in a setting where I am sharing my memories that someone hasn't said "that reminds me of a time..." Do you see how that works?

Another way to get the memories flowing is to start a memory writing group (this has so many benefits!). What seems to concern most people is whether or not they can pull enough stories from their memory bank to make it worthwhile. Several years ago I was meeting with a group of people every week for another purpose and decided to ask if any of them would like to get together once a month for the express purpose of "memory writing." There was lots of interest so I then challenged them to write one memory in the next month and bring it with them to share at the next meeting. From that first meeting I knew I was onto something. We heard stories from one lady who was a child during the German occupation of Holland in World War II and how she survived, another told about losing a sister as a result of her hair catching fire from the candles on their Christmas tree (long before there were such things as electric lights for Christmas trees), another told of her mother walking barefoot through the Rocky Mountains just to move her family away from the brutally cold winters. That same day we heard amusing stories that made us laugh until we could barely breathe. A memory writing group accomplishes several things:

1. It helps you get to know the other members – you learn things you would not likely get to know through casual conversation and deep friendships develop.

2. As people share their stories, memories of your own come to the surface.

3. It motivates you to keep writing.

4. It gives you ideas of how to put your own memories together for your family (do you have them bound into a book, do you include your genealogy, etc?).

Your memories and stories are there, it just takes a little prodding to bring them to the surface so you can write about them.

Included with each chapter is a **Memory Example**, **Food for Thought** and a list of **Memory Triggers**. These examples will help you understand the value of using descriptive words, details, humor and facts in your memory writing. Also at the end of each chapter is a **Notes** section. This provides a place to jot down some notes of your own memories that will come to light as you read this book.

 **Memory Example:**

Chocolate Covered Cherries

Mother and Daddy were really struggling financially in 1947. If my memory serves me right, Daddy was working for $.50 a day in Iowa doing really hard work and it just wasn't enough to feed, house and clothe a family of six.

Aunt Frieda (Daddy's sister), Uncle Helmer and their only son Jacob, had moved to Boone, Colorado where Uncle Helmer started an electrical business. Somehow they got wind of the fact that our family was in real trouble, so they wrote to my folks and generously offered Daddy a job. They even offered for us to live with them until the folks could get on their feet.

Daddy had suffered with asthma all his life and, once they moved to Colorado, his asthma seemed to clear up, a secondary benefit for moving west.

When Daddy was a teenager, his dad (my Grandpa) became ill with tuberculosis. In those days, everyone knew that dry climate was better for that particular disease so they moved from Tennessee to Colorado because there was a tuberculosis center in

Colorado Springs. That facility was on the grounds of what is now the University of Colorado at Colorado Springs.

With that in mind, they decided to accept U. Helmer and A. Frieda's offer. What they didn't know was that U. Helmer and A. Frieda were living in a very small three room house. The rooms were no more than 8' x 10' each. There was running water in the kitchen but no sanitary facilities at all. At that time, indoor plumbing was only for the rich and there were only a couple families in that category in Boone in 1947. Everyone had outhouses. Bathing time was once a week - Saturday night. We used the wash tubs that were used when doing laundry. Ours were round and I've often wondered how the adults managed - obviously they had their legs and feet hanging over the side. Everyone wanted to be the first to bathe because they didn't change the water between baths. Order of bathing was how dirty you were - meaning little girls (especially the littlest one - me) usually went first. That was the only time you had an entire room all to yourself but because so many were waiting their turn and the fact the water did NOT stay warm, bath time only lasted long enough to get the job done.

Boone was a very small town. Water was scarce so no one even thought about having a lawn or flowers. If there were trees, they came up volunteer. The thought of planting trees that you had to water was unheard of. Weeds did tend to grow with no water so the project of keeping them under control was assigned to the younger children.

We must have moved to Boone in the fall of 1947 and we lived with U. Helmer and A. Frieda through our first Christmas. Daddy worked for U. Helmer and somehow they managed to scrape enough money together to buy each one of us a box of chocolate covered cherries for Christmas. Oh my goodness! My own box of candy. I thought I had died and gone to heaven. We rarely had candy and to have my own box - it was one layer about 8" long by 4" wide - seemed too good to be true. I think we opened them all at the same time and I remember just staring at mine. I think Philip and Rachel dove right into theirs, but Susan and I didn't. I'm not sure how long Susan kept hers, but I didn't open mine for what seems like the longest time. I'm not sure whether it was days or weeks but when I finally opened my treasure and took a bite, I was a goner. I ate the entire box in one sitting! Well, my little system (remember, I was only 4) was not used to anything like that - it was used to very basic food and not lots at any one time and so sure enough it rebelled. I was not blessed with savoring the last bite and looking back on my box of chocolate covered cherries with fond memories. From that day to this the thought of eating chocolate covered cherries turns me "green."

Food for Thought: How many things can we learn from this story?

1. Where the family was living before the move
2. It places Daddy in Tennessee when he was a teenager
3. The year of the move
4. Reason for the move
5. Wages earned in 1947
6. To what state the family moved
7. Family connection of people offering their home
8. The living conditions
9. How many lived in that home
10. Age of the memory writer at the time of the event
11. Description of the town
12. The occupation of the uncle
13. Illness and allergies in the family
14. The facility previously on the grounds of what is now UCCS…a little history of Colorado Springs
15. Christmas in the year 1947

Many of these details are very important historically because it tracks the family from one state to another with critical dates. This story also describes the living conditions that may seem "impossible" to the generations reading it. It may give the children and grandchildren a new perspective of Mother's/Grandmother's early life.

 Memory Triggers:

- **Adventures** – horseback riding (whose horse, where, what happened, what kind of horse, how big), auto accidents (what happened, who was driving, where were you), getting lost, finding a deserted house…

- **Automobiles** – describe the ones your family had, give year, model and color, were they used for pleasure or strictly as a necessity?

- **Awards** – name them and then describe why and how you received them

Notes:

"I Could Never Write Like You Do."

Remember who you are writing for. You're probably not writing the next "Little House on the Prairie" stories. Not everyone (including me) is a Laura Ingalls Wilder. Write as if you are telling a story. When you talk to your friends and are reminiscing about the "good old days" do you worry about whether you can tell a good story? Of course not. One of the highest compliments I ever received was when one of my childhood friends (after reading my first set of memories) said, "Lana, I couldn't put your book down. It just felt like you were sitting beside me telling the story. I could hear you talking as I read." She could not have said anything that pleased me more. Use your own personal expressions. I often take what I call "writer's privilege" and use exclamations or underlines, even though I know that an editor would probably be tearing their hair out. Your memories are for you and your family. Write them from your heart and let your words flow. Along that same vein of thinking, if you are from a section of the U.S., or perhaps from another country, and speak with an accent, use that accent in your writing. It doesn't always have to be grammatically correct when you are telling or writing a story. What you want your readers to hear is your voice coming through your words, so, if Grandpa used to say something unique to him, include it in your story. It will seem much more special and personal to your family as you make yourself vulnerable in your writing.

 **Memory Example:**

The Spanking

I must have been about 3 years old because this event happened before we moved to Boone in 1947.

Church has always been a major part of my life. Perhaps it stems from the fact that I had such an early introduction. I'm not sure of my age when the folks took me to church for the first time, but I suspect I wasn't more than a few weeks old. In those days, when women gave birth, they were expected to rest for several weeks before resuming their normal activities and I doubt if Mother was any exception. I was a big baby weighing 9 lbs. 14 oz. at birth – I'm not sure how long I was but Mother at her peak was never more than 5'3" so you can imagine what it must have been like to carry and give birth to such a big baby. Susan was ten years old and Rachel was seven so Mother had two good helpers while she was recuperating. I was born on May 2, 1943, at St. Joseph's hospital in Memphis, TN.

By the time I was three we had moved from Memphis to DesMoines, IA where the spanking took place.

Daddy was a deacon in the church we attended in DesMoines. I don't know if the deacons were expected to sit in the front of the church during all of the services or maybe it was communion Sunday that put them there. All I know is, on this particular Sunday, Daddy was sitting in the front with a whole pew full of deacons. It may have only been 3 or 4 but to me it seemed like many more.

Mother, Susan, Rachel, Philip and I were sitting somewhere close to the back on the right side of the middle aisle. I have no idea how large the church was but to a three year old it seemed big. Mother had her hands full with Philip and me both so young (he would have been two) but for some reason we were not in the nursery. Perhaps there was no such thing – I'm not sure. At any rate, right in the middle of the service I decided I wanted to sit with Daddy. Without saying anything to Mother (which probably means I knew I would have been deterred) I jumped down off the pew, ran right down the middle aisle straight for Daddy. My memory says he was sitting at the end of the pew and the look on his face left no doubt that I was in BIG trouble. He took one look at me, shook his finger at me and told me to "get back to Mother." I'm sure both of them were horrified beyond description. I didn't hesitate! I turned around and went straight back to where I had come from. Mother said, "you are going to have a spanking when we get home." I was terrified and sat like someone in a straight jacket for the rest of the service. I had never had a spanking to that point but I knew it was going to be bad.

I don't remember the ride home. I just remember Mother had me by the hand when we got out of the car and she didn't even put her Bible down when we got there. I'm thinking the basement must have been more of a cellar than an actual basement. There were stairs leading down to it and that's where we went. There was a stool or chair down there and Mother said to me, "this is going to hurt me a lot more than it will hurt you; but, you must understand that you cannot leave where you are sitting in the middle of a church service, so I'm going to spank you to help you remember."

She then told me she loved me and laid me across her lap. I think she only used her hand for the actual spanking but I thought I was not going to survive. I think it was probably no more than 4–5 whacks but it seemed like an eternity. When it was over and I looked up, tears were streaming down Mother's face.

I decided right then and there, from that moment on, I would try my best not to make Mother that sad ever again. That decision (as young as I was) kept me out of a lot of trouble as I was growing up. When I was tempted to do something I knew was wrong or that would eventually bring sadness or grief to Mother if she found out, I just didn't do it. That resolve kept me out of a lot of dangerous situations and I've never regretted it.

I don't believe (and Mother concurs) I ever had another spanking.

 ## Food for Thought:

1. This family went to church
2. The father was a deacon in that church
3. The recipient of the spanking was very young
4. It places the event in DesMoines, IA – to where the family moved from Memphis, TN
5. It loosely describes the basement/cellar
6. Corporal punishment (not abuse) was used
7. The spanking had a lasting impact on the writer's future decisions

 ## Memory Triggers:

- **Birthdays** – did you have cake and ice cream? Was the ice cream homemade? If so, describe the ice cream maker. Where did you get the ice? What was your favorite kind of cake? Did you have candles on the cake? Did you have a party? Was there ever a special birthday gift that you still remember?

- **Bomb Drills** – why did the officials think they were necessary? What were they like? Were you afraid?

- **Childhood** – start with your earliest memory and be prepared as they come flooding back.

Notes:
_____

"This Seems Like Too Big Of A Project."

I felt the same way. Every time I thought about it I shivered. Many of you probably finish every project you start and never have nagging thoughts in the back of your mind of "some day I'll get started on that." But there are those of us who do not fall into that category and I'll confess that my nemesis is the drawers and boxes full of unmarked and unorganized pictures that need to be put into albums, given to my children, put on DVDs or tossed. Had it not been for one small idea, the "memories project" could have fallen into that genre.

In January of 2005 I decided to start writing one memory every week. For years, when trying to remember my childhood memories, very few came to the surface. Naively I thought I would be really stretching it to come up with 52 memories (spanning my entire life) to give to my children for Christmas 2005. I didn't tell anyone about my project. I didn't want to get any hopes up in case I couldn't remember enough or something came up preventing me from completing this goal. I didn't even own the goal as "mine" – just in case. But I was in for a delightful surprise! The more I wrote, the more I remembered. (In an earlier chapter, I suggest you keep paper handy to jot down memory topics as they come to mind). By the end of January I had a list of 52 memories to write about and I was only up to AGE 10!! My project proved so exciting that it took all of my willpower to come home after work and not head for the computer. Now the memories flow when I'm in the car, at work, in the grocery store, at the movies, cleaning house or baking cookies. There's something about the aroma of fresh baked cookies that brings stories to mind. For me, baking is an especially good activity to entice memories to come forward.

It takes me approximately one hour to write each memory. That is one hour a week. As busy as I am, one hour seems "doable" to me – and it is. There are weeks when I write two or more memories – especially when I know I have a busy week ahead of me, or I'm going to be gone, etc. I like to stay ahead a couple of weeks so that when the fall comes, I'm not under a lot of pressure to get number 52 completed before the end of the year. Frankly, I love writing my memories so much that I look forward to the opportunity each week to sit down and write. It is never drudgery.

 **Memory Example:**

Thumb Sucking

We must have been about five and six years old. I had always sucked my thumb and Philip had always sucked his middle two fingers. There were no such things as pacifiers and the normal age for getting rid of such habits was much younger than we were.

Mother and Daddy had tried to discourage us from this habit but nothing seemed to work. I don't remember them making too big of an ordeal about it, I just remember them encouraging us to take our thumb/fingers out of our mouth any time they saw that we had them in there.

Uncle Tim and Aunt Claudia came from Iowa to Boone for a visit. One of the first things they wanted to see was the mountains. Aunt Claudia grew up in Memphis, TN, moved to Iowa and had never seen the Rocky Mountains up close. Uncle Tim had been in Colorado along with the rest of his family when Grandpa Bruce had tuberculosis, but had not been back here for a long time.

One of the closest drives we could make that wouldn't take all day was to the towns of Rye, Beulah and Lake Isabel – all southwest of Pueblo. They are about 1-1/2 hours away from Boone.

The Beulah Highway (as the natives called it) was a stretch of two lane, paved, straight road out in the middle of nowhere. In 1949 there was very little traffic - in fact to this day there is very little traffic (comparatively) – but beautiful views of the foothills leading up to the Rocky Mountains.

At one point Aunt Claudia was so in awe of what she was seeing, she asked if we could stop while she took some pictures. Of course all of us bailed out of the car and were standing alongside the road while she took the pictures when all of a sudden a state patrolman appeared out of nowhere. I guess we were so enthralled with the picture taking escapade we didn't see him coming. Anyway, he stopped and said, "make sure you keep the children away from the traffic," and started to move along when

18

Aunt Claudia said, "wait, we have a little boy and girl here who suck their thumb and fingers; you want to take them with you?" Well, Philip and I were absolutely terrified!!!!!!!! We started running as fast as we could go, climbed into the car, got down on the floor and covered our heads with our hands. Of course the patrolman said, "no thanks, just keep them off the road." But Philip and I didn't show our heads for miles and miles – we didn't want him changing his mind. From that moment on, we NEVER put either our thumb or fingers in our mouths. Of course, it gave us such a fear of policemen that it took YEARS to overcome that horrible feeling. Anytime we saw any kind of law enforcement officer we either hid behind Mother's skirt or ran the other way.

One day when I was 14, a policeman came into the shoe store (B & A Bootery) where Mother and I were buying shoes. I began to shake and wanted to leave the store; however, Mother decided enough was enough, took me by the hand and walked right up to that policeman and said, "my daughter has a terrible fear of anyone in uniform, would you please talk to her and explain what you do and why you do it?" He talked to me for several minutes explaining how they are there for our protection and how, if I obeyed the law, I would never have to worry or fear them. It was the beginning of my journey to freedom where law enforcement officers were concerned.

 Food for Thought:

1. Family history with Memphis, TN
2. Childhood habits
3. Childhood fears
4. Sightseeing opportunities in Southern Colorado
5. Extended family visits
6. A little history of the aunt and uncle and their draw to Colorado
7. Grandpa Bruce's illness
8. How the writer's mother dealt with the writer's fear of policemen

 Memory Triggers:

- **Children** — When did you start having children? Describe how you felt as soon as you realized you were going to become a parent. Where were you, who was your doctor? Did you have baby showers? If so, who did that for you and where were you? What did they use for decorations? Did anyone build a cradle or other heirloom for you? Where were your children born? If you were in a hospital, how long did you have to stay there? Were you in a private room or a "ward"? Describe your children's birth order, their personalities or as much as you can remember about each one. Tell where they were born, when they took their first step, got their first tooth and how you chose their names. Tell some of the humorous things they did or said - you could write a separate book or section for each one.

- **Chores** – did you have any? How old were you? Give descriptions.

- **Churches** – name the ones you were a part of. Where were they? How did they help develop your spiritual life? Name the preachers and describe their families. How big were the churches? Did your parents ever invite the preacher and his family into your home for a meal? Were they full time or did they have another job? Tell about Sunday School, possibly singing in the choir, teaching Sunday School or Vacation Bible School. Was there a teen group? Describe some of the kids in the group. Did you ever go to church camp? What was that experience like? How far was your camp from home? How long did your camp last (one week, two weeks…)? Did you make new friends at the camp?

Notes: _____

_____

_____

_____

_____

_____

_____

_____

_____

_____

_____

_____

_____

"I'm Afraid My Siblings Won't Remember The Stories Like I Do."

It is a legitimate, natural concern to think you may not remember an event exactly the same way as your siblings, but it is your memory for your family and I believe you should write the story as you remember it, not the way someone else remembers it. One of my sisters is 10 years older than I am and the other one is seven years older than me. If I am writing a story that took place when I was six years old, that would mean one sister was 16 at the time and the other one would have been 13. There is no way all three of us will remember the event exactly the same way. As soon as my siblings found out about my first set of memories, they wanted to read them. Well, I could see the writing on the wall. I knew they had their own versions of past events and frankly, I was not interested in how they might want to change some of the details as they remembered them. So, I told them they were welcome to read my memories as long as they didn't try to change anything. If they wanted to "set the record straight" they would have to write their own memories (which I encouraged them to do). They agreed to just read and enjoy what I was writing. Each of them have copies of my stories and now, when we get together, we enjoy discussing some of the events I've written about that they may have either forgotten or were not important to them at the time. Sharing your stories with your siblings can be a wonderful reconnecting point. Especially when you begin to write about the years after you left home. You will be surprised at how many of your memories will be new to them.

 **Memory Example:**

Rain Storms and Wiggly Things

Philip and I rarely took anything "with a grain of salt." If the good Lord presented an opportunity to play, who were we to miss the chance?

Boone, Colorado was a very hot, dry little town. Unless the ground was prepared for a lawn or garden, it was as hard as stone. The streets were dirt – not gravel or brick like some of the surrounding towns but dirt – rock hard dirt.

Although the Arkansas River was just two miles to the south of Boone, the normal humidity was usually below 10%. There was no Pueblo Reservoir and the nearest lake was 30 miles east of town in Ordway. The farmers north of Boone made their living with a method called "dry land farming." Over the years they learned how to preserve every drop of moisture or dew that fell to the parched land throughout the year. They knew when to furrow the land after the harvest in the fall, and when to disk it in the spring before planting time. Those dry land farms were really very large ranches – many of which had several thousand acres of land. They also raised cattle on their land – several hundred head of Herefords every year.

Usually, each summer we got one or two storms. Because Boone had such flat terrain, we watched the storms coming – usually from the West (over the mountains) but sometimes from the East. The clouds built up, turned black and about the time they reached Boone they unleashed their fury. The lightning lit up the sky as the dark thunder clouds rumbled. The wind roared and then the rain poured – sometimes for quite a while. The dirt was so dry and hard there was no way the moisture was going to penetrate it as it rushed down the street. There was a ditch about 3 feet wide and 3 feet deep right in front of our house and during those storms that ditch filled up with rushing muddy water.

When the storm passed, Philip and I ran out into the yard, with our pant legs rolled up and shoes off, to play in the mud puddles. The dirt was clay and when it got wet it squished between our toes and stuck to our feet. Sometimes it built up so thick we had to scrape it off with a stick just to keep playing. Every living creature in Boone enjoyed the rain. It made everything smell good and look clean. It washed off the dust and dirt from the leaves on the trees and bushes so they looked brighter and usually a deeper puddle or two stuck around for several days. The frogs and crickets sang to their heart's content. The frogs laid their eggs in those puddles and just about the time it looked like the puddles were drying up completely, the eggs began to turn into tadpoles and it looked like the mud was actually wiggling. We would locate some kind of container (usually a tin can) put water in it and rescue those tadpoles. They swam around in our cans and within just a few days, began to sprout legs and feet – back ones first and then a few days later the front ones came. About the time the front ones came the tail fell off and they were ready to be dumped out of the can. If there was still damp mud around, that's where we dumped them. Otherwise, we used our own water and made a damp puddle for them. From that point on we didn't see them again but, as they matured, we heard them sing in the evening and we knew we had been a part of saving them from drying up before they had a chance to become frogs. To this day, I love to hear the frogs and crickets sing in the evening in the summertime.

Food for Thought:

1. The proximity of the Arkansas River to the small town
2. The climate of Boone, CO years ago
3. Description of the soil
4. What the rainstorms meant to the children
5. The process of tadpoles becoming frogs
6. One way the children entertained themselves
7. The explanation of "dry land" farming

 Memory Triggers:

- **Clubs or groups you were active in.** How old were you when you were in the club or group? What was the purpose of the group? Did it have a name? What were some of the activities/trips you took with that group? How big was the group?

- **Discipline** – what (if any) forms of discipline did you receive and why?

- **Driver's License** – how old were you when you started driving? Who taught you to drive? What kind of vehicle did you drive first - tractor, car with manual or automatic transmission? Did you learn to drive in the country or in the city? Do you remember taking the test? Were you nervous – especially with the driving part? Do you remember some of the feedback of the person who rode with you for the driving part? What was your first car? Was it given to you or did you pay for it? What color was it?

Notes:

"Do I Have To Use A Computer Or Can I Handwrite My Memories?"

Whether you write your memories with a pen/pencil or type them into a computer is strictly up to you. There is something special about memories written in your own handwriting. I have an original set of memories handwritten by my mother and they are a real treasure. My children have asked that I handwrite some memories, so I eventually will. However, for now, it is much easier for me to use the computer as I do a lot of editing when I write and I want the end product to be neat and tidy without a lot of erasing or, worse yet, words crossed out. Although I try to write in sequential order, if I remember another event that needs to be inserted in a different position, place or page, it is much easier to make that change on the computer.

It is amazing how many opportunities will come your way once people hear about your project. Having everything on the computer in one file makes it easy to print one or several memories if you get a request from someone. For instance, I was approached by a Grandparenting network to use one of my memories in their publication. Having the entire first edition on the computer made it very easy to write an introduction to the article, then just cut and paste the memory to link to it. Another thing to consider is the number of requests for copies of your memories you will receive. Relatives and friends will be interested in your stories and having them on the computer makes it very easy to print a copy for those people.

 **Memory Example:**

Christmas

Christmas was a special time at our house. Mother and Daddy worked hard at making it that way.

There was always a Christmas program at the church. It usually consisted of the little choir singing carols and, as someone read the story in Luke 2 about how God sent His son in the form of a baby, that same story was acted out on the platform. There were children dressed up as shepherds, wise men, Joseph and Mary and cardboard camels, cows and sheep. The manger with straw and a doll were always in the center of the stage. I don't think I was ever asked to be Mary – I think I would remember if I had been. Anyway, after the program, we went downstairs (to the unfinished basement) where paper bags filled with candy, fruit and nuts were passed out to all the children. These "gifts" were usually tied with either red or green curly ribbon. That was the closest thing to the secular part of Christmas that was allowed at Calvary Baptist Church. There was never a Christmas tree or lights – they really wanted the focus on what Christmas was all about – not what the "world" wanted it to be.

This particular Christmas had to have been after Susan and Rachel were married and no longer living with us. It seemed that once those two events happened, although Mother and Daddy were always ready to help either one of them when they needed it, things began to improve as far as cash flow was concerned. Mother was working at the school running the lunch program and she worked at the Post Office four hours a day. Daddy had a good job at the Pueblo Ordnance Depot (later to be called the Pueblo Army Depot) working on the Nike Missile Program.

I don't remember requesting a bicycle, but Philip and I both must have been asking because, low and behold when we got up Christmas morning, there were two shiny bicycles in front of the Christmas tree. I cannot begin to describe my excitement. Up to that point, everywhere we went was on foot. I don't remember having a tricycle when we were little, we ran (rarely walked) everywhere. If we needed to run an errand for one of the folks, that is exactly what we did. We ran. Sometimes that meant running to the grocery store – which meant two blocks south, across the railroad tracks, across Highway 96 into the store, getting whatever was needed and then reversing the same route. I'm not sure – in fact I doubt – we were required to run – we just did.

Until recently, I thought both of us had brand new bicycles. However, after discussing it with Philip, he says his was a used one – previously owned by one of our brothers-in-law. He can tell that story. Mine was new and I LOVED it! There was no such thing as hand brakes at that time. You came to a stop or slowed down by using the pedals. I rode it EVERYWHERE! When I had an errand to take care of, I rode my bike. There was no basket on the front, so I carried whatever I went after in one hand and guided with either the other hand or my legs. To have my own bicycle was something my friends didn't have. Usually there was one bicycle per family and they took turns sharing. Since I had my own, I gave my friends rides on mine. They sat on the back bumper and held their feet far away from the wheel and away we went. More than once, they didn't listen when I told them to hold their feet out and sure enough, their feet got tangled in the spokes of the back wheel bringing the bicycle to a halt and both of us crashing to the hard ground. It never was a pleasant event. It hurt. We were always on dirt or gravel roads and, when we landed, we usually got up with bleeding knees, legs, arms, elbows and hands.

I loved that bicycle. I could go much further and faster than walking or running. It wasn't long before just riding was not enough. By now you know there was some dare-devil in both of us and this was a perfect opportunity to see how far we could push the limit. The road in front of our home was on a slant. Not a hill really, because Boone was pretty much flat, but a definite slant. We rode to the north end of the road – which was the top of the slant. We'd then start down that "slant," get going as fast as we could until our feet couldn't keep up with the pedals, then put our feet up on the handlebars, let go with our hands and go "flying" to the bottom of the road. We eventually got to where we seldom used our hands for hanging on. We could guide with our knees and let our arms and hands just hang to our sides or if we were trying to impress anyone that might have been watching, put our hands behind our heads.

There were no rules about wearing protective gear –the pedals hurt my bare feet so I think most of the time I wore shoes.

There were lots of dogs in Boone. I think almost every family had one – except us. Mother didn't like them and Daddy hated to hear them bark so we didn't have one that we could actually call our own. At one point, Daddy brought home an injured stray and nursed it back to health (I can still recall the smell of the stuff he used to put on his wounds) but then he got rid of it. Anyway, dogs were not the favorite pet of our family.

The neighborhood dogs loved to run along beside us when we were on our bicycles. And for the most part, other than a yap or two, that is just about all they did – just run alongside. This particular day, I took one of my girlfriends home after we had played all afternoon. Her name was Raylene and she lived about four blocks east of us. Coming back, I was almost home when the neighbor's dog came running at me and decided to take a chunk out of the back side of my knee. I was close enough to home that Mother and Daddy heard my scream, shot out the back door to see me *lying in the street beside my bicycle. It was a fairly large gash, one that was going to require stitches. They wrapped my knee with a tight clean rag, put me in the back seat of the car and we headed for Fowler to see Dr. Thomas. Of course his first remark was, "we have to quarantine the dog to make sure it is not rabid." That didn't faze me until he further explained that if rabies were involved, I would be in for a series of very lengthy, painful shots and probably hospitalized. Well, that scared the liver (and probably any infection) right out of me. So much so, that I barely remember him taking care of my knee except that there were no stitches involved. Instead he used the newest thing – staples. I got a lot of attention with those staples – none of my friends had ever had staples and they watched every day for when they would fall out. Sure enough, after about two weeks, that is exactly what happened and I wear the scar to this day. Obviously the dog was not rabid, he was let out of the pen after two weeks and I continued enjoying my bicycle right up until I was old enough to drive a car.*

 Food for Thought:

1. Description of the Christmas program in a small country church
2. Occupations of parents
3. Description of bicycles
4. No protective gear
5. Only dirt roads – no sidewalks
6. Acrobatic Stunts – fear was not an issue and dealing with pain was just something everyone endured
7. No pets in the family
8. Treatment of dog bites

 Memory Triggers:

- **Entertainment** – what did you do for entertainment as a family or by yourself?

- **Family Genealogy or Family Tree** – this information can be included in your memory book if you wish. It can be as simple or as complex as you want it to be.

- **Fishing** – Fly? Deep sea? Lure? Bait? What did you like to catch? Where have you fished? Describe some of your fishing trips. Hunting - for what? Did you use a gun? What kind? Bow? Where did you go hunting? Where did you stay? In a tent? In a cabin? Motel? Camper? Back of your pickup truck?

- **Friends and Neighbors** – were you close? Did you get together often? Did you help each other? Did your family have "best friends"? Did they have annoying pets (barking dog) or beautiful gardens? Did they have children your age? What were their living conditions?

Notes:

"Do I Need To Copyright My Work?"

If you are going to share completed copies of your memories, it might be wise for you to copyright your work for your own legal protection. Too many innocent, generous people have been left out in the cold when someone helped themselves to something they had written but didn't protect.

Don't let this discourage you from writing your memories for your family; I mention it for those who may receive requests for copies of their stories from extended family members or friends. If your work is original, it is presumed to be copyrighted and anyone who tries to infringe on it will have to prove it is not your work. Copyrighting your work is not as complicated as you might think. Contact the U.S. Copyright Department in Washington, D.C. or at uscopyright.com for instructions on the process.

 **Memory Example:**

Uncle Carl's Bunk Bed Adventure

We had many visiting relatives. All of our relatives thought we lived in the "wild, wild west" and they wanted to come see how we were "surviving." We loved having them come. By the time this particular event happened, Mother and Daddy had it "down." We always took our guests from out-of-state to the Royal Gorge, Phantom Canyon, Victor, Cripple Creek, Manitou Springs and back to Boone – all in one day.

Our visitors this summer were Uncle Carl, Aunt Alice, Ronnie and Bonnie. Ronnie is six months older than I and Bonnie is not quite one year younger than Phillip.

As always, we planned our big one day adventure. We always looked forward to this particular excursion because you never knew what you might see or do along the way. If you have been to the Royal Gorge, you know that there is an admission charge once you get close to the bridge. However, if you have no interest in crossing the bridge or going to the gift shop, or if you cannot afford those things, there is an area that has been fenced off so you can lean over the fence to see the bridge and canyon with the Arkansas River far below. We NEVER paid to see the bridge. We ALWAYS stopped and looked over the fence; which was chain linked about three feet high so we children were held onto very tightly to make sure we didn't do something crazy and wind up going over that fence.

The day went just as planned. Uncle Carl always liked to stop in the tiny town of Victor, Colorado at the end of Phantom Canyon for Cherry Cider. It was usually dusk by the time we got to Manitou Springs and we made it a tradition to stop at the Red Top Cafe on S. Nevada for the biggest hamburgers served anywhere before we drove back home. It was a beautiful day with lots of fond memories to keep us awake for a long time after the lights were turned off for the night.

We had two sets of bunk beds in the one bedroom. My sisters Susan and Rachel may not have married yet. They may have even accompanied us on this excursion. I'm not sure about that, but I do know that Uncle Carl and Aunt Alice slept in one of those bunk beds this particular night – with Uncle Carl in the top bunk.

Everything was very quiet. We children were sleeping on the floor in the living room after talking and giggling for what seemed a deliciously long time before being told to be quiet and go to sleep. The entire household was sound asleep when, all of a sudden, a horrible racket came out of the bedroom where Uncle Carl and Aunt Alice were sleeping. Of course, Mother and Daddy were out of their bed and into that bedroom almost before their feet hit the floor and what they found was Uncle Carl on the floor! He had been sleeping on the top bunk. What could have possibly happened? Did the bed fall apart? No, everything seemed to be in order. He was sort of moaning and groaning and finally awakened enough to tell the story. He had been having a nightmare that Rachel had fallen over the fence at the Royal Gorge and he jumped over to save her. Of course, when he jumped over, he actually jumped out of the top bunk in our house!! Once everyone knew he was alright, there was much frivolity over the entire situation and it probably doesn't have to be said – sleeping was over for the night for the entire group! It is a memory the entire family remembers and talks about almost every time we get together – even all these years later.

 Food for Thought:

1. Relatives involved
2. How those relatives pictured the family living in Colorado

3. Sight seeing route

4. Historical restaurant

5. Particular "likes" of family member (Uncle Carl liked cherry cider)

6. Type of beds in the children's bedroom

 Memory Triggers:

- **Funerals** – when did you go to your first one? What was your impression? Was it in a church? Who was it for? What was the service like? How did you feel at the time? Who (if anyone) gave you comfort?

- **Games** – what inside games did you like to play (board games, cards, dominoes)? What outside games (Hide 'n Seek, Kick the Can, Annie Annie Over, Cowboys and Indians)?

- **Gifts you received** – what made them special enough that you can remember and write about them?

Notes:

"How Do I Keep Track Of The Memories I've Written?"

For the most part, your stories will probably be "stand alone" – it will be rare when one story leads into another. To organize your memories, name and number each one and have an index with the titles and numbers in the front of your book. This is a good way to reference your stories when you are talking about them to others. For instance, if someone wants to know about the "Horseback Riding" adventure in my book, all they have to do is go to the index and look up that particular story, instead of trying to remember, "now was that memory towards the front, in the middle or toward the back of the book?"

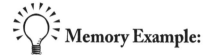 **Memory Example:**

The Sweet Peas

Daddy loved to garden and it was not long after he built the house that he staked out a small space between the back porch and the street for ours. I'm not sure whether the garden or front lawn came first but, in those days, if you put any fence in at all, it was in the front yard, not the back. It was a chain link fence – there was not a wooden fence in town – no one had them. The idea was not for privacy but more to keep the critters from getting in the yard and eating what was growing in the garden or digging up the yard.

The idea of a flower garden was not what Daddy had in mind. A garden was to help provide groceries to put on the table. This was a small garden – large enough for radishes, green onions, carrots, beets, tomatoes and that was about it. No cucumbers or melons – not enough room for that nor was there enough water. He separated the garden and the lawn (which not only was in the front of the house but also along the south side of the house) with a small wire fence.

Mother's idea of a garden was not necessarily to grow vegetables, but to have a spot for flowers. So they compromised. Every March, Mother planted annual sweet peas at the base of the fence that separated the garden from the lawn and, by the time school was out, just before Memorial Day those sweet peas were in full bloom. Sweet peas are my favorite flower. I don't know if it was my early introduction to them or what, but it still warms my heart if I can have even a sniff of a sweet pea sometime during the summer. There are many different colored annual sweet peas (perennials are usually pink) and they were beautiful blooming on that fence in our yard. The more you pick them, the more they bloom – a wonderful thing for a child who LOVED having a few in her bedroom or sitting on the table in the kitchen.

There was a little girl named Abby (who had several problems at birth) born to the Shafer family in Boone. She was unable to walk, speech was difficult and reading almost impossible. Abby had several siblings. They lived on the north side of the train tracks like we did and I don't remember what the dad/husband did for a living but it never seemed to us that they had very much in the way of worldly possessions. They were a good, moral family really undergoing some hard times. It took everything Mrs. Shafer had just to care for her family. In those days mothers cleaned the house (rarely with a vacuum) mostly with a broom or dust mop and dust rag, did laundry with wringer washing machines and rinse tubs, (getting the water in and out of those things was a huge task) hung the clothes on a clothesline outside to dry (that meant that when you brought them in the clothes were so stiff they could practically stand by themselves and very wrinkled – mainly because everything was 100% cotton – which meant you had to sprinkle them with water, roll them up and let them stay that way for several hours before you ironed them), cooked and baked everything from scratch, kept up with all the school work and activities, did any yard work there was to do including the garden, canned fruits and vegetables in the fall, kept everyone clean, made most of the children's clothes and probably lots of other things I'm forgetting. Mrs. Shafer did all of those things while trying to care for Abby.

One summer day (I couldn't have been more than 8 or 9) Mother suggested that I pick a bouquet of sweet peas (I used a pint jar for a vase) and take them to Abby. She also suggested I take one of the books from the bookmobile and read to Abby. This would give Mrs. Shafer a bit of a break and might even be a "ray of sunshine" to that family by showing them that people actually cared. I loved the idea and wound up doing that very thing several days a week during one entire summer. I absolutely loved my visits with Abby. I had to give the sweet peas a day or two to re-bloom between picking but as soon as there were enough for a bouquet I was on my way. The Shafers lived just a couple blocks from our house and there certainly was no danger of my walking there and back (on the dirt street) by myself, so that was my summer project. Over the years when our paths have crossed (Abby is still in a wheelchair) she always recognizes me and asks if I remember the sweet peas. How could I ever forget?

Food for Thought:

1. The different definitions of "a garden"
2. Description of the Shafer family
3. Expectations of a wife and mother in those days
4. Mother's soft heart for people in the community
5. Mother used sweet peas to teach the writer the life lesson of thinking of others
6. Describes why the writer loves sweet peas

 Memory Triggers:

- **Habits** – ever suck your thumb or bite your nails? How long did you do that and how did you get free of the habit? Describe other habits you might have had.

- **Holidays** – were there certain foods that you always had on holidays? What did you do on specific holidays? Did you go for a picnic on July 4th? Were there fireworks? What about parades? Did you always have a Christmas tree? If so, where did you get it and what did you use for decorations? If you did not celebrate Christmas, what were your family holidays and how did you celebrate? Describe them.

- **Homes** – how many places have you lived? Did you move a lot as a child? How did that affect you? Did you live in the same home your entire life? How did it feel when you finally moved out? Describe some of the homes, yards and neighborhoods where you lived.

Notes: _____

"Do Men Ever Write About Their Memories?"

Y ou bet men write their memories. Women do not have a monopoly on memory writing. Some of the best stories I've heard were written by men. One of the first questions my children asked after reading my first edition was, "Where's Dad's?" It is just as important for families to understand why Dad/ Grandpa does the things he does or who he is, as it is for them to understand Mom/Grandma. Daughters/granddaughters love to read about their Dad/ grandfathers - what made him thoughtful, tender, kind and loving - while sons/grandsons love to read about all the wild, crazy and daring things he did. I am always thrilled when a man joins our little memory group. My first thought is always, "their family is going to be so pleased!" It's a win/win.

I currently work for a church and one of the responsibilities of my job is helping people with the memorial service when a loved one passes away. When we meet with these families, it is very common for them to want to talk about the deceased – sometimes a particular story; other times just memories in general. They may say something like "Dad had such a rich life" or "he was always looking for the next adventure" or "he could keep you in stitches with his stories." If the opportunity is right, I often ask (with much delicacy) if they have those adventures recorded and I'm always pleased when the answer is in the affirmative. However, many times I don't even have to ask. I know the answer and that family will live the rest of their days with those stories lost forever.

 **Memory Example:**

Butchering Day

Living on the farm had many advantages. Our food was always fresh, had no preservatives and we had a great variety. Dad and Mom were from very traditional families so we didn't have a lot of extravagant meals. Just "good old home cookin'" was the best way to describe it. Mom was a good cook and baker. We always had cookies and an occasional pie or cake.

Our vegetables were raised on the farm and we put them up in canning jars or froze them. Dad bought a huge chest freezer so there was adequate space to keep the frozen foods. He also built a pantry in the basement that had lots of shelving to store the canned goods.

This brings up one of the significant events that happened each fall. Butchering day!! There were usually three different days that we did this. One for chickens, another for beef and another for pork.

In the spring, Dad went to the feed store in Pueblo and purchased 100 baby chicks. He brought them home and put them in the chicken house. They were separated from the bigger chickens under a "brooder" hood that used infrared lights to provide warmth for the baby chicks. As the chickens grew, (which was usually pretty quick; within a few months they were as large as the adults) we separated the young hens (pullets) from the roosters. On butchering day we took a number of the roosters and some of the pullets, if there were more than we needed for laying eggs, and butchered them. We then put them in the freezer for use when we wanted fresh chicken.

Dad also made a pig pen out on the back of the building site and we usually had an old sow. She bore piglets in the spring and we let them grow, sold a few and then butchered one or two for our own use. We bred the milk cow or purchased a calf and raised it for beef. We let the animals become yearlings so they were full grown when we butchered them for meat.

On butchering day, my Grandpa, Grandma and Aunt Molly came out from town, and sometimes a neighbor, and/or other uncles and aunts came to help us. I'll spare all the gruesome details of butchering, but it was always a great time to work together as family and put up the food for the next season. We had roasts, steaks, hamburger, ribs, pork chops, whole chickens and chickens cut up into fryers. There was always plenty of good fresh meat.

One of my vivid memories of butchering day is when Grandpa removed the brains out of the skull of an animal and fried them with scrambled eggs. I don't know if I would eat this today, but it was fun to be the brave young boy who tried this experience when my cousins would not.

Dad also purchased turkey chicks from the feed store and we raised them for Thanksgiving and Christmas dinners. We usually had 25 turkeys and we shared them with family and sold some of them to family and friends.

One of my favorite memories was working with Grandpa. He always came out to the farm to help us on butchering day. It was quite an experience.

 Food For Thought:

1. Writer lived on a farm

2. The family raised their own meat – chickens, pigs, cattle and turkeys

3. The family butchered their own meat

4. Friends and relatives came to help

5. Friends and relatives were treated to some of the meat

6. The family raised and sold turkeys for the holidays

7. Chickens and turkeys were bought as chicks

8. The writer describes how they kept the chicks warm while they were too little to survive on their own

9. The family raised their own vegetables and canned them

10. The family had a freezer for their meat

 Memory Triggers:

- **Hospitals** – why were you there? Recovery? Doctors? Describe the hospital. Were you afraid? Did the nursing staff make you feel comfortable? Were you allowed visitors? Were you in a private room or a "ward"?

- **Instruments** – did you play a musical instrument? If so, which one(s)? Did you play in the band or orchestra? Where did you perform? Were you interested in music? If so, what kind? Who were your favorite "movie stars"? Did you have a radio? What did it look like? What stations did you listen to?

- **Interests** – sports - which sports did you play? Did you have uniforms? What did they look like? Talk about your coaches and team mates. Are there special sporting events that you remember? Cheerleading – were you ever a cheerleader? What were your school colors and what did your uniforms look like? Sewing - did you take sewing in school?

What did you make? Cooking - who taught you to cook and when? Any flops or successes? Farming - what did you raise (chickens, pigs, cows, crops)? Did you have a barn? Did it have a hay stack? What was that for? Did you milk the cows by hand? Gardening - do you like to grow things to eat or flowers – why? Art - sculpting, oils, charcoals, pencils, landscapes, portraits, scenes?

Notes:

"Can I Include Pictures?"

By all means, include pictures if you have them. If you are doing this project on the computer, scan your pictures and then place them into your document at the places where you think they fit the best. Your family will love them. In fact, many times the picture you choose to fit the memory may spur them on to actually read the memory. If your pictures are old, cracked, black and white – so be it. You are more than likely telling very old stories so no one should expect the pictures to look like they were taken yesterday. If you are hand writing your memories, take the pictures to your local office store and have them make the copies for you.

 **Memory Example:**

First Performance

During the year I was five, Mother was the president of the PTA (Parent Teacher's Association). This group was very active back then. It was a major part of the town's activities – even for those who didn't have children attending school.

School funds were always an issue so there were several opportunities during the year to help bring in extra money. Due to the fact that there were so many Mexican families in the Boone community, and also that they were good cooks, the PTA sponsored a Mexican dinner every year. There are certain wonderful smells that take me back to those dinners even now. They really were feasts. Those women made hundreds of tortillas, tamales, tostados, enchiladas and tacos. Everyone in Boone and neighboring towns showed up for it year after year. I still respect the amount of work that went into that event. Not only all the cooking, but there were no paper/plastic plates, utensils or drinking cups, and there certainly were not enough glass ones for everyone, so they had a team of people who did nothing but wash dishes for hours and get them ready for people coming in as people were going out. They cooked for days. They had to do that after the noon meal at the school lunchroom because, every morning, full meals were prepared for most of the students attending all 12 grades of school. They didn't have freezers or microwave ovens. Everything was made from scratch every day. Many times lunch was the only full meal that some of the children had for that day. Mother was the head cook for several years and of course we didn't think there was an unpalatable meal served. She was a great planner and had learned how to budget from her childhood. There was always a main dish, vegetable, usually a salad and some kind of dessert – often homemade pies. They served an average of 60/70 meals to students and teachers five days a week so the Mexican women had to plan their preparation time for the Mexican dinners in the afternoons and evenings.

I don't know if there had been any musical productions performed before Mother and Daddy came to town but I believe that is one of the first things Mother decided to do after she was elected president of the PTA. I don't remember the name of the musical but I do remember what a big production it seemed to me. It was a negro spiritual and everyone came from miles around to see it. The gymnasium was packed with people from wall to wall. Remember reading about how shy I was? Well, Mother decided Philip and I should sing in this musical; not with anyone else, just the two of us standing in front of about 400 people. We sang "Mammy's Little Baby Loves Shortenin' Bread." Philip was 4 and I was 5. We were blackened from head to toe with some kind of black grease, my hair was braided in tiny braids all over my head and, with knees shaking, he and I walked out onto that stage holding hands and sang for the first time in public.

I've often wondered if that was Mother's and Daddy's way of helping me overcome the shyness. One thing I do know, it awakened something in me that said I loved to perform – either on stage in plays and productions, singing in groups, playing in the band or marching in competitive drill teams.

 Food for Thought:

1. Writer's age
2. Introduction of the PTA
3. Multicultural environment
4. Fund Raising took place "way back then"
5. Description of the food served at the Mexican Dinner Fund Raiser
6. What was done before the invention of disposable dishes or plasticware

7. Mother was the head cook for the school lunch program

8. Description of a school lunch and how many were served

9. Introduction of entertainment for the Mexican Dinner through the PTA

10. Why the writer sang

11. Explanation of future performing tendencies

 Memory Triggers:

- **Jobs** – What was your first job? Where did you work? How much did you earn? What were your responsibilities? Do you remember your boss or how long you worked there? Did you have a job description? Was it full-time or part-time?

- **Laundry Day** – did you use a washing machine or scrub board? Describe hanging out the clothes…any particular "hanging order"? How about starching, dampening and ironing them? When did you get your first automatic washer/dryer?

- **Military** – in what branch did you serve? What was your rank? Where were you stationed? Write about boot camp. Did you serve in any wars or conflicts? Were you injured? Talk about your recovery. Who were your buddies? Did you have "kp duty"? Write about the food – did you like it? How long was your tour of duty? What did you do in the service? What was your title? Where did you travel? Did your military service include the Reserves? Were you married or single when you enrolled? How about when you mustered out?

Notes: _____

_____

_____

_____

_____

_____

_____

"Do I Have To Know My Family's Genealogy?"

Although it can be a wonderful addition to your work, it is not necessary to include your family's genealogy or family tree. Some people thrive on digging into their family history, learning about their family's place of origin, who they are related to and what their relatives did. However, it is not at all necessary to include that information in your stories unless you want to. If you are trying to share your life experiences with your family, don't get so wrapped up in your genealogy that you neglect to share your rich, fascinating stories. My memories do not go back past my grandparent's generation, so my stories start there. I have a sibling who loves to do genealogy research so I'm happy as a clam to let her. I'm not downplaying the necessity of tracing and recording one's genealogy, but your stories should be relational and personal.

 **Memory Example:**

Playing

I'm not sure how soon after we moved into our new home that Daddy built the back porch. I'm thinking it must have been one of his first projects because that was where we kept the washing machine. Once the porch was finished it created an "L" onto the east and south sides of the house.

Cowboys and Indians was pretty much the "play of the day." After all, we lived in the "wild west" and it hadn't been all that long since cowboys and Indians actually lived or roamed the area we now called home. You could walk not more than two blocks from our house and be in open range land. If you paid attention and looked carefully, you could find authentic Indian arrowheads. In fact, many farmers and ranchers in the area to this day have extensive, authentic arrowhead collections.

There was no television when we were little but there were books, comic books and radio that opened our imaginations to what it must have been like just a few decades before our play time. In fact, it was still such a prevalent part of our culture, our first school writing pads were called Big Chief and had a picture of an Indian headband on the front.

To work on the house, Daddy made several sawhorses. These sawhorses were constructed out of 2" x 4" lumber. The legs were about three feet high (there were four of them) with a cross piece in the middle. They were sturdy enough that you could lay a piece of plywood across them and do whatever cutting you needed to do. Or you could lay a piece of plywood on them and use it for a platform if you needed to work on something high.

Philip and I decided we could make a restaurant in the "L" of the house. Since two real walls had been provided, we used those sawhorses to outline the other two walls – making sure we left an opening for the doorway. We used wooden crates for the table and sitting area. The whole thing was probably 10' x 12'. The idea was that I ran the restaurant while he (being the cowboy) took care of the Indians. We scrounged around until we found several sizes and shapes of tin cans we thought would work for dishes and then I began to make mud pies. The dirt in Boone was very hard clay and it took LOTS of time just to get it soft enough to use by digging with shovels and sticks. There was no such thing as plastic spoons and Mother and Daddy certainly didn't have anything old enough that was unusable. It never entered our minds to take something from inside the house to use outside just for "play." Because water was so precious we filled up one discarded tin can with water and made it last just as long as we could while making our mud pies. Once filled, I set the pies out in the sun to "cook." It didn't take long. It was not unusual for the outside temperature to be over 100 degrees in the summertime.

Once we got the frame for the restaurant constructed, Philip took off on his "horse" which was a stick about 3' long. He was usually gone quite a while and I'm not exactly sure what he did during that time but he always came back hot, sweaty, tired and ready for whatever the restaurant had to offer. He sat at the "table" and made up stories about what he had just seen or done while I busied myself with getting him something to eat – which meant prying the mud pies out of the tin cans.

All of this took place on the east side of the house. The porch supplied shade from the south side making a perfect "L" for our play time. In the heat of summer it was a very cool, welcoming place and sometimes Mother even brought real lemonade out to help cool us off.

We spent hours and hours playing in our restaurant for several summers. It is a memory I cherish.

Food for Thought:

1. Daddy built their home which included a back porch
2. Description of the shape of the back porch
3. Back porch included the laundry room
4. The family lived in the "west"
5. "Cowboys and Indians" games were prevalent
6. Description of school writing pad covers
7. Concept of collecting authentic Indian arrowheads
8. Life without television
9. Description of how these children spent their time
10. Description of a "sawhorse" and what they were used for
11. Description of the dirt in the little town
12. How they "made do" with tin cans and sticks
13. Water was scarce
14. Climate in their town – temperature was hot in the summertime with very little rain

Memory Triggers:

- **Pets** – did you have any? If so, describe what they were (breeds and species), their antics and how you or your family felt about them.

- **Play** – what did you do? Did you need others around you or were you content to play by yourself? Did you like being outside or would you rather play inside? Did you have a favorite game or games? Did you have a favorite teddy bear or doll? How about a favorite wagon or fire truck?

- **Politics** – who was president during your childhood? Was your family active politically? Did that help form some of your current political affiliations? If so describe. Did you watch or experience any cultural changes?

Notes:

"What About Copies Of Legal Documents?"

If you have historical documents, include them if they relate to the subject matter of your story. For instance, if you will be writing about when you got married, feel free to include a copy of your wedding certificate, or if you are writing about the birth of your children, include copies of their birth certificates. Use your imagination – the sky is the limit. I have a book on childcare and nutrition that I put together when I was in Jr. High School and I hope to insert some of that book in the section when I write about that point of my history.

 **Memory Example:**

California

The summer of 1954 – we had a brand new, light blue Ford and $500.00 in our pocket. I didn't know where the funds came from until years later. I just knew that all-of-a-sudden we were headed for California for vacation, which was not unlike Mother and Daddy to surprise us with a trip. Several times during my childhood I came home from school to find Mother and Daddy packing the old metal suitcases saying, "We are going to Newton, Iowa for a few days." However, the idea of going to California was a really BIG deal in my 11 year old eyes.

Mother and Daddy tried to give us nice things, all the while scrimping pennies every place they could. Knowing we would be crossing the desert and since there was no such thing as air conditioning in automobiles yet, the next best thing was a portable air conditioner that hung on the outside of the car window. It was tubular shaped about the length of the car window. You filled it with water and the forward motion of the car (plus whatever mechanical devices were on the inside) forced the cooled air into the car – similar to what is now called a swamp cooler. I think I also remember some kind of a chain so if you wanted a quick mist all you had to do was pull it. We only did that at the hottest point of the day – most of the time we just let it blow the cool air into the car. The plan was to only stay in a motel one night coming and going. Mother and Daddy knew Philip and I would probably get antsy just sitting in the back seat for the long drive, so Daddy put a piece of plywood between the back of the front seat and the back seat the same height as the back seat. Then they put blankets and pillows on that board. We could lie on that board and not squish whoever was sitting on the back seat. We slept there, but we also read and colored while lying on that board. It was great. Seat belts had not even been thought of. Mother always packed food on our trips. We rarely stopped at a restaurant while we traveled. One particular evening (I'm assuming the first evening because we ALWAYS started REALLY early – no later than four a.m.) we stopped in the desert. I don't remember it being particularly hot, and my memory says Arizona; however, since the weather was mild, it might have been New Mexico at supper time. Daddy built a small fire ring out of rocks that Philip and I gathered together - no fire restrictions back then - and Mother had brought corn on the cob and potatoes wrapped in foil which she cooked in the coals of the fire. Philip and I could hardly eat for fear Indians would come swooping down on us at any moment. It seemed as if we were out in the middle of nowhere, so why not? Daddy was very "into the trip" – I can't help wondering if he fed our imaginations "just a bit" that evening.

When we arrived at Aunt Eunice and Uncle John's, it was as if we had entered another world. They lived in a small but adorable Spanish style home. The outside exterior was very rough plaster painted white. Their yard was impeccable. Lots of flowers and bushes. Even the sides of the yard next to the house were landscaped – unheard of in Boone where we lived. The small living room walls were each painted a different color. I think I remember one rust colored wall, one was dark turquoise, another was light green and I believe the other was an ivory color. The ceiling was shiny silver – I've often wondered how they achieved that affect because it looked like aluminum foil. I seem to remember the garage in the back and it was as spotless as the house.

So much to see and do – it was hard to grasp everything. Uncle John and Aunt Eunice were terrific hosts. They wanted us to see as much as possible because the idea of any of us ever returning was almost unthinkable. The day they took us to the beach was one I'll never forget. It was a warm, beautiful day. I remember my first look at the ocean and couldn't wait to jump in.

One particular event regarding my swim in the ocean was that I nearly drowned! Daddy had gone quite a ways out; Mother and Aunt Eunice were not far from me. Knowing I couldn't swim they tried to stay close. Who knows where Philip and Eddie (our cousin) were but I'm guessing somewhere close to Uncle John. I was up to probably my waist in water and I spotted what looked to me like an enormous conch shell (the kind you put up to your ear and hear the ocean) lying on the ocean floor. I dove for it, got caught in the rip tide and was immediately rolling over and over not knowing which way was up and way over my head. Aunt Eunice realized I was in trouble and swam to reach me. Just as she got there I surfaced, saw her and made a lunge towards her. She was very small in stature and when I grabbed her we both went down. Now we were both struggling. I don't know when Daddy realized we were in trouble, but the next thing I remember is his strong arms pulling me back up to the surface. As soon as I felt his arms I let go of Aunt Eunice, and since she could swim, she had no trouble getting back under control. Daddy helped me get into water shallow enough that I could touch the bottom, and then he insisted I walk back to shore with him right beside me. I'm sure that was his way of making sure I "got right back on the horse" and I thoroughly enjoyed the rest of the day playing in the water close to shore.

The other thing I remember about that day is that there were small, booth like restaurants all along the beach. These restaurants were no more than 10' x 12'. You walked up to an ordering counter, got your meal and sat down on the beach to enjoy. The one we stopped at was selling deep fried shrimp. I thought it was probably the best thing my taste buds had ever encountered. The smell of the oil in which the shrimp were cooked has been unforgettable. I would recognize it even today; however I have never encountered that exact aroma since that day. I'm sure all the ambience of the moment has something to do with it – the salt air, smell of the ocean and then the shrimp cooking - added up to something that will not be duplicated in my lifetime.

Another place showed to us was a memorial grounds/cemetery/mausoleum named Forest Lawn. The only cemetery I had visited was in Fowler, CO. The one in Fowler was right out in the middle of the prairie, east of town – no lawn, no trees and only gravel on the road. I was in for a shock when I saw the breathtaking Forest Lawn area. It felt like paradise instead of a cemetery. As we entered the grounds, my memory says it was so full of trees that it seemed almost dark (like a forest) with a beautiful, well-manicured lawn that wound around between the trees and bushes. As we entered the small, intimate chapel nestled between the trees and large bushes, no one had to say "be quiet" to Philip, Eddie or me. It was (and has been) one of the most serene experiences of my life. I wondered if Jesus was going to walk in and take a seat on one of the dark wooden pews. Each stained glass window told a story and I could have spent hours in that place. I think there are some very famous people buried in Forest Lawn. I'm thinking one or more *presidents of the U.S. and maybe a movie star or two but I was not nearly as impressed with that as I was with the beauty and serenity of the entire place.*

After we left Forest Lawn, Uncle John wanted us to see Hollywood. Of course the mansions were almost more than I could actually "take in." It didn't seem real or authentic – the houses sat far back off the streets and the grounds of each one were immaculately groomed. I kept thinking no one could possibly live there until Jack Benny himself stepped out his front door and waved to us. I thought Uncle John was going to jump out of the car. From his reaction I'm sure he never expected that we would actually see a real, live movie star but there was Mr. Benny picking up his newspaper like any normal human being.

Knott's Berry Farm was a wonderful day as well. It had been established just a few years prior to 1954 and definitely had a western flair. There is at least one picture, if I can get my hands on it, of Mother and Aunt Eunice being silly on a bench outside one of the frontier stores. I don't remember the rides. I'm not sure there were any at that time but one of the things I do remember is the Knott's Berry Farm jelly. To eat out was always a special treat and that's what we did that day. There was a sit-down restaurant connected to the General Store and there were shelves and shelves of more varieties of jelly than I had ever seen for sale, both in the restaurant and the General Store. Most of them were made from boysenberries, (thus, Knott's BERRY Farm) which I had never heard of.

After we had been sightseeing one day, the plan was to eat at home that night. I know it was planned because Aunt Eunice had prepared a tamale pie ahead of time and that was the main dish for dinner that night. Again, both Philip and I LOVED that tamale pie. It is one of the few times I have been tempted to actually make a pig of myself at a meal and it took every ounce of self-discipline in my entire body to show my manners. Either we were extremely hungry or it was the best tamale pie to ever be served. She had black olives in it, as well as corn and spices. We NEVER had olives at home so that was a real treat; however, I'm convinced that no one before Aunt Eunice or after her could make a tamale pie tastier than the one she served to us that evening.

Another highlight was our trip to Catalina Island. Catalina is an island 26 miles off the coast of Long Beach, CA. We boarded what seemed to me to be a cruise ship (I'm sure it wasn't but it certainly was no small boat – at least not to me) and headed out to sea. I remember standing on the side of the ship watching the "flying fish" skim above the water right next to the ship. Uncle John obviously knew what to watch for and made sure we saw them. When we got to Catalina we boarded a glass-bottomed boat for another ride out to sea. This time we didn't go nearly as far but we watched the fish in the sea through the glass bottom. Divers swam under the boat with food for the fish luring them so we could all see and enjoy them. They were beautiful – what a special day for our family.

All good things must come to an end and our California visit ended all too soon. Daddy wanted to see Las Vegas so we took the route that led to that city on the way home. I'm not exactly sure why Daddy wanted to see Las Vegas because our "visit" lasted less than 10 minutes if my memory serves me right. We drove down the strip once – which was NOTHING like it is now – a few cheap motels is all I remember, and then we drove out of town with what few bright lights there were flashing in his rear-view mirror. To my knowledge, Daddy never returned. It did not fit into his idea of morality or spiritual convictions and he wanted no part of it. I remember thinking, "what was that all about?" I'm still wondering...

At some point on the way home, out in the middle of nowhere (which was most of the trip) I was sleeping on the board between the seats. All of a sudden Daddy hit the brakes, came to a screeching halt, said, "You kids stay in the car," and he and Mother bailed out of the car. As I sat up, Philip was saying, "it's a wreck." The roads were all two lanes - each direction had one lane. An oncoming car pulling a camping trailer had lost control, swerved the trailer right in front of our car, then swerved right behind our car and, when it swerved back into their lane, the car and trailer toppled over. In a matter of seconds, several people came crawling out of the car unhurt. Mother and Daddy were right there and several other people stopped. With no one hurt, the main need was to get the vehicles back up on their wheels. It was probably going to take a wrecker. No one had cell phones so the discussion was directed toward who would go on and call the police and who would stay with the family until the police and wrecker got there. Daddy volunteered to call the police at the next town. For years after that, when the discussion came around to what kind of a recreational vehicle Mother and Daddy would have once they retired, Mother always said, "no trailer – camper or motor home but no trailer."

There was a surprise when we got home, road-weary but still basking in the glow of a fantastic vacation. We walked into the kitchen and there on the counter next to the stove was a line of tiny, black ants. Thousands of them! I'm not sure how it happened, but there had been just a few grains of sugar left on the counter when we cleaned up the kitchen for the last time before we walked out the door and the ants found it! There was a line of ants in a long row coming into the house, across the *counter straight for the sugar. Then there was another line (each ant followed the other — very orderly) going back across the counter and outside. Horror of horrors!!! It was not hard to find their home — they led us right to it. All Daddy had to do was follow those lines and he made quick work of those ants — at least once they were outside. Mother and I very quickly started getting rid of them inside. It took several days for them to stop coming, but from that point on, I've checked and rechecked the kitchen counter for grains of anything before leaving my home for any extended trip.*

That trip to California was one of the highlights of my childhood. I will be forever grateful that we had the opportunity for that kind of vacation. I believe it bonded the four of us even closer together. Mother and Daddy never wanted us to waste as much as a minute. Mile after mile we either sang together, recited the states and all of their capitals — beginning with Washington and ending with Florida, played "My Grandfather Runs A Grocery Store," recited poetry or spelled. Our trips together were never boring and I looked forward to every one.

 Food for Thought:

1. Age of the writer
2. Destination of this particular family vacation
3. Concern of parents regarding driving conditions
4. Description of the window air conditioner
5. Parents making even the meal time an adventure
6. Who the family visited and what their home looked like
7. The near drowning of the writer
8. Lasting aroma of the beach and food sold at restuarants
9. Description of Forest Lawn Cemetery
10. Special meals and why those memories linger
11. What was lurking at home when they got back and why the writer has always left her house very clean before a trip

Memory Triggers:

- **Reading** – did you read as a child or did someone read to you? If so, what kinds of literature did you like? Did the Bookmobile come in the summer time? Were you in any kind of reading club? What kept you motivated to read? Was there a library in your town and did you enjoy browsing through the aisles deciding which book(s) to check out?

- **Relatives** – favorite (or disliked) aunts, uncles, cousins. Where did your grandparents live? Describe their visits to your home or your visits to their house. What do you remember about them? For instance, did your grandfather smoke a pipe or cigar? Do those scents bring back memories of him? What did their home look like? Was it in the city, town, country or on a farm?

Notes:

"What If My Children And Grandchildren Don't Want To Read My Stories?"

It would be naïve to think that your children and grandchildren are just waiting for you to write your memories down for them and will "drop everything" to read them. To be honest, I'm not sure all of my children, their spouses and my grandchildren have read what I've written. In fact, I'm fairly certain they haven't, and that's okay with me. You might ask, "After all the work you put into recording your memories, doesn't it hurt your feelings or disappoint you?" I had to think about that long and hard before I started writing. I looked at my relationship with my parents and grandparents and had to come to grips with some of my own attitudes when I was busy raising children, working, etc. The need to know the stories of my parents and grandparents wasn't as acute then, as it was once I became an "empty nester" and had time to think about my roots. The same may happen with your family - they may not read your memories until years from now. Don't let that discourage you. At some point, they are going to want to know what makes (or made) you tick and they will have your stories to help them figure that out.

 **Memory Example:**

Found/Lost Treasure

As most children, Philip and I had our share of curiosity. We loved to explore our surroundings and although they were sparse compared to today's neighborhoods, we didn't seem to have any trouble keeping ourselves occupied. Our imaginations were very active. We loved to hear a good scary story. It was deliciously fun to be scared half out of our wits and to know we would be safe and secure in the end.

We were not supposed to wander south of the railroad tracks, but anything north of the tracks was pretty much fair game. We knew that side of town like the back of our hand. We knew every tree, bush and weed. We knew where the tack burrs, yucca and tumbleweeds grew and, oh yes, the devil's claw weed. You haven't lived until you've picked a devil's claw weed. (It has claw-like vines [for a lack of a better word] about six inches long that curl around and look like something wicked). We new which houses were occupied and which ones weren't. We knew if "crazy people" lived there or if they were "nice people." We knew if they were the town gossip or the preacher. We knew what nationality they were, how many people lived there, what their dad did or didn't do for a living and could usually tell you what they were having for dinner just because they left their doors and windows open most of the year with the exception of a few cold, winter months.

Directly across the street to the south of our home (the streets were not named) was a large two story house – at least it seemed big to us. There was always a lot going on in that house. Sometimes the preacher lived there, sometimes large families lived there and sometimes it was the meeting place for what we called a "holy roller church service." It never was officially named the "holy roller" church but they made a lot of noise while they worshipped and our little neighborhood was not used to that. In that little town, if you didn't attend one of the two Baptist churches or the Catholic Church five miles up the road in Avondale you were "weird." They sang loud and made LOTS of noise. Philip and I used to think we could see them climbing the poles in the middle of the room in some kind of a ritual. Needless to say, we were not allowed to attend so we just let our imaginations run...

On the other side of that house/church was a small little shack that, years before, had been someone's place of abode. I don't think I can actually call it a home. It really did look like something straight out of a western movie. One day Philip and I decided we had waited long enough; it was time to explore that shack. To our surprise, the back door was unlocked and we walked right in. We probably weren't older than 5 or 6 and we were pretty nervous about the whole thing. We knew we should not be in there – it didn't belong to us. There was a table, a chair or two and a kitchen cabinet. We opened that cabinet and found a tin container. Well, our curiosity was in high gear and we opened the container. LOW AND BEHOLD THERE WAS MONEY IN THERE! Oh my, you can imagine our excitement. It seemed like a small fortune. If my memory serves me right, it was about $20.00. We were RICH! We couldn't wait to tell Mother and Daddy! We spent that money a hundred different ways on our way home. We knew no one lived in that house and, as far as we were concerned, that money belonged to us.

You can imagine the look on Mother and Daddy's faces when we got home. Believe it or not, they did not punish us with the normal spanking – they did something MUCH WORSE! They decided to call the Pueblo police department to see if anyone had reported any money having been stolen or lost. Of course they had not. That money had been there for years and long forgotten in that vacant shack. They told Mother (she made the call) that they would hold it for a time and if no one claimed it, they would return it to us. We never heard from those policemen. I'm fairly certain they went out to dinner or to the bar that night with OUR MONEY! We never went back to that shack. I'm not sure why Philip never went back, but the reason I didn't was the fear of finding more treasure and not being allowed to enjoy it!

 Food for Thought:

1. A little geography of the town; location of railroad tracks
2. Description of some of the weeds (which would indicate the part of the country where this event took place)
3. Types of churches in the area
4. Description of the little shack and proximity to the writer's home
5. Discovery of the treasure
6. Mother and Daddy's ethics in turning the treasure into the Police Department
7. The disappointment of "losing" the treasure

 Memory Triggers:

- **Modern conveniences** – did you have electricity? What kind of heat was used in your home? What kind of stove did your mother use for cooking? When did you get your first telephone (describe the party line if you had one)? Television - (was it only black and white)? Did it have rabbit ears or antenna? What were your favorite shows? Were you only allowed to watch so much each day or certain programs? Did you have running water or modern bathroom facilities? How about hot water?

- **Parties** – did you have parties while you were growing up? If so, what were they like and how frequent were they? Were your guests relatives or friends or both. Were your parties inside or outside? Did you play games/cards? Describe.

- **Performances** – were you in school, community or church plays? Where did you perform? How did you feel? Why did you do it and what characters did you play?

Notes:

"How Did You Know What To Write About First?"

Because I'm a sequential thinker, it made sense to me to start with my very first memory. That doesn't mean the memories started flowing in order from that point on. I'm still not sure I have them in the correct order from so many years ago but that is not the most important thing. The most important thing is that they have been written and hopefully they help explain why I do what I do and who I am to my family. If at some point you get "writer's block," pull out those grandparenting books sitting on the shelf and let some of the questions help you start remembering again. So far, I haven't run into that problem - and I doubt you will either - but it is a resource "in your back pocket" if you need it.

 **Memory Example:**

My First Memory

My very first memory is a birthday party – I don't think I could have been more than 3 – maybe younger because I was 4 when we moved to Colorado and in my memory, it was much earlier than that.

The party was for a little girl who lived around the corner from us but, because there were no fences back then, you could go out our back door and cut across the yard to her house.

I remember really looking forward to the party, probably because it was my first one, but also because there was not much occasion for parties in 1945/1946. It must have been after we moved back to Iowa from Memphis, TN. We were poor, but so was everyone else. Adults were trying to recover financially from the Great Depression and emotionally from World War II.

I don't remember any grass in the back yard – just dirt, clothesline, outhouse and stuff that accumulates when there is no garage. There may have been weeds in the neighbor's back yards; however, there were none in ours. For as long as I can remember, Daddy never tolerated weeds. The minute one sprouted and was spotted, it was pulled and destroyed. Burning was allowed back then so we always had one or two old, rusted, round metal 55 gallon oil drums that we put our trash, or anything we wanted to destroy, into. For years, there were no lids for the trash barrel. Lids came later when we "moved up in the world." Anyway, that is where the weeds went and when they were dry, we burned them. When the barrel filled up with ash, Daddy hauled it to the country, dumped it out and brought it back. That is also the way we disposed of all the household trash. Tin cans took a long time to become ash.

Back to my story...I was a very shy little girl; the type who hid behind Mother's skirt when we were around anyone I didn't know. We didn't have many elderly people in our lives at that time and certainly no one who was "different" – meaning anyone with a disability or even anyone who had a foreign accent. I was very frightened of anyone who fit these descriptions.

As I remember, Philip and I held hands, with me carrying our gift, and very timidly walked across the back yard. The house where the party was to take place was two levels with a basement so we walked up what seemed like mountains of white stairs and knocked on the door. A tiny, white haired, wrinkled grandma answered the door. Well, I was expecting our little friend to answer the door. I took one look at the elderly lady, screamed at the top of my lungs, dropped the gift and Philip's hand, left him standing there, and went running as fast as my little legs would go back home. Mother heard my screaming and met me at the door. Philip went on in to the party (and I'm assuming had a great time – I think he even brought me a party favor and piece of cake) but I never went back – not that day or any other. Mother tried to ease my fears and get me calmed down but could not convince me to go back. She told me she would go with me, she talked to me about the sweet little grandma, etc. but my mind was made up and I missed my first birthday party.

 Food for Thought:

1. This story places the family either in Iowa or Tennessee, for historical recording

2. The writer was very shy

3. It places the year sometime after WWII

4. Everyone was struggling financially

66

5. It describes the yards

6. It describes trash removal or disposal

7. It talks about the writer's Dad's aversion to weeds and his meticulous nature

8. Describes the "no fence" culture

 Memory Triggers:

- **School Days** – Describe your first day of school. How old were you? What did your school look like? Was it a one room school house? Was it built of brick? Was there a lunchroom? Did you eat the lunches prepared at school or did you take your lunch from home? If you took it from home, who prepared it and what kind of container was used (i.e., paper sack, metal lunch pail, etc.)? Talk about the teachers you remember and why you remember them. What did you do for recess? What kinds of grades did you get? What subjects did you particularly like or dislike and why? Did you participate in any school sports, debate teams or musical or drama activities? Explain. Did you graduate? Describe what that looked like.

- **Schools** – how many did you attend and where were they?

- **Siblings** – How many and who? How old? Are/were you close? Did they teach you things? Did you like or dislike foods just because one of your siblings had the same inclination? Did you look up to the older ones or take care of the younger ones? Describe things you did together as children.

Notes: _____

_____

_____

_____

_____

_____

"What Did Your First Book Look Like As A Finished Product?"

Take some time and think about what you want your end result to look like. You want to make your book appealing so your family will want to read it, right? These days there are countless products that will help you create an attractive book. The variety of letterhead stationery and decorative paper is almost limitless. I like to try to match the paper with the story. For instance, when I wrote a story about why flowers are so special to me, I chose stationery with a floral border; I put the story about the rattlesnakes at the ranch on western paper. Use your imagination. If it seems like too much trouble to match paper and memories and you feel you are doing good just to get the stories written, use plain white paper. The cover can be anything you want – preferably something that will be a reflection of you. I've seen covers that were simple (and yet quite elegant) - a beautiful rose on a black background, a picture of a favorite painting, or a family photo that depicted the time frame of the book. My first book has a black and white family photo with me as a toddler because it covers the first ten years of my life and introduces the family into which I was born. My second book has my high school picture on the cover, the one after that will have a wedding picture on it. Be creative, it's your book of memories. Maybe you have written an edition of all sports memories - put several pictures of you participating in sports on the cover. If your memories have a theme of music or drama, put something that supports those activities on the front, or perhaps you want to draw something that depicts what the book is about. The sky is the limit! The cover should somehow relate to what your readers have to look forward to and it will help preserve your stories.

Depending upon how fancy and intricate you want to get, there are many places on the internet where you can get a fairly inexpensive, hard bound cover for your book. You can also take your book to your local office store and choose a three-whole punched cover with a clear sheet on the front for your book. The store will three-hole punch your book for you. This protects your work and gives it a finished appearance. I recommend this process for your first project as it will be easier to add something to it later, if you need to, without damaging your original project.

I also recommend you make more than one copy of your project. Several years ago I had the privilege of reading the life story of someone who had her memories and family history bound in a hardcover book to be given to her family after she was gone. She wrote it when she was in her 80s, was then in her 90s, and her family had yet to see her book. It was delightful, but after reading it I could see where each of her family members was going to want a copy and it would be difficult to accomplish this without damaging the original. If you have several children, make sure you make copies for each one to avoid initiating an unintentional family feud.

 **Memory Example:**

Centipedes, Black Widows, Tarantulas and Rattlesnakes

This may come as a surprise ☺ *but Boone was not a thriving, well developed town. Not exactly a "frontier town" – it did have electricity and running water – but fairly rough around the edges; it was not uncommon to either see or hear of a tragedy. If we were in dark or damp places, we watched for black widows and centipedes. If we were in hot, dry areas, we watched for scorpions and rattlesnakes. To this day I rarely put on a pair of shoes without turning them upside down and giving them a good shake.*

Centipedes have 100 legs. At the end of each leg is a little stinger. One morning our neighbor put on a pair of slacks and there was a centipede about 6 inches long in one leg. As soon as his leg met the centipede, all those little legs and stingers went to work. He was very ill for many weeks but he did recover completely, as far as I know.

Mrs. Miller lived in the block just south of our house. She was a tiny little thing and, in my mind, was older – although not ancient. One fall day while putting on her sweater she was bitten by a black widow spider that was lurking in the arm of that sweater. She did not recover – in fact she passed away because of that black widow's bite.

One summer I was spending some time with Susan and Cody on their ranch, before they had children, and Susan had located a spot in one of their fields where she thought she could raise a few vegetables. I'm not sure why she picked that particular area or how she got the water to that area-whether she took it in buckets, or she might have located a spring; at any rate, she had several thriving yellow squash plants that were producing squash better than I knew was possible. "Thriving" is almost an understatement. Those plants had LOTS of sunshine out on that ranch and they loved it. They were big – maybe six feet in diameter. Susan decided she and I needed to go pick some squash for dinner. We drove to the field; I jumped out of her pickup with my bucket and headed for the squash. I was enjoying being with my sister and not really thinking about any danger. I spotted a large squash plant and, without even looking for danger (which was rare – because we had been taught to be alert), I began to extend my arm into the plant when I heard a rattle. Sure enough, there was a rattlesnake, coiled, head up and preparing to strike. Had my hand been a fraction closer, I probably would not be writing about it today. I pulled back just in time, and instantly was running and screaming across the field, with Susan standing there wondering what in the world was the matter with me. We went back to the house. I never picked squash with her again and I don't know if she ever planted anything in that area again. Rattlesnakes were a common thing to see or hear on the ranch, but she may have decided that squash picking was too dangerous and providing them with a nice cool sanctuary from the summer heat was not her responsibility.

The street in front of our house seemed to be in the migration path for tarantulas. Black ones – about 3 inches in diameter; sometimes brown ones which were much smaller. Every spring they came from the hills north of town and walked down our street like they were on parade, on their way to the Arkansas River which was about two miles south of Boone. Every fall they made the trek back from the river to the hills. We sometimes caught them in jars and took them to school – most of the time we just let them continue on their journey.

Another spider incident occurred when I was 12 or 13. I went to bed one night and, just as my head hit the pillow, I felt something crawl into my ear. It freaked me out! I ran into Mother and Daddy's bedroom and told them what was happening – I could feel it moving around deep inside my ear. Mother said, "just go back to bed, put the same side of your head on the pillow and maybe it will crawl back out." That was one of the hardest things I ever had to do. I lay there for a long time, feeling it trying to find its way out. It finally did. The hardest part was once I felt it heading in the right direction, lying perfectly still until it got all the way out for fear it would get frightened and head back in. Once it was out and I raised my head, there it was, lying on my pillow, about ¼" in diameter and black. I don't think I slept much that night.

You may be beginning to get the picture of some of the things we had to deal with as just a "normal" way of life. We didn't know any different. Everyone in Boone experienced the same things. It taught us to be constantly aware. We couldn't be inwardly focused or have "tunnel vision" - we HAD to know what was going on around us at all times. Our lives depended upon it.

71

Food for Thought:

1. Several tragedies related to the topic

2. Description of a centipede

3. Brief description of the living conditions in Boone

4. This story helps explain the writer's healthy respect/fear of spiders and snakes

Memory Triggers:

- **Swimming** – where did you learn to swim? Did you take lessons? Did someone throw you into the water so you had to swim to survive? Where did you swim - public pool, private club, river, irrigation ditch, lake or ocean? Did you ever water ski? Where? How old were you? Whose boat did you use?

- **Teen Years** – describe your friends and activities. Were there school dances or proms? If so, what did you wear? What about other activities? When did you start to date? Did you have a teen idol - who was it and why? Did you ever get to see or meet him/her? What kinds of movies did you like to go see? Did you ever go to a drive-in theater? Did you ever get an autograph from someone famous? Did you wear uniforms to school? If so, describe. If no uniforms were required, what did you wear? Were the girls allowed to wear pants or jeans?

- **Time** – how did you spend your free time? With whom did you spend it? Were you artistic? Were you sports-minded or were you a "tomboy?" Did you have the chance to let your imagination run free and "invent" things to do?

Notes:

"All Of My Childhood Memories Are Sad."

If all your childhood memories are sad, my heart goes out to you and I'm very sorry. So...maybe you don't start with your childhood memories. Maybe you write about when you met your spouse, or when your babies were born. What was it like to hold them in your arms for the first time? How did you choose their names? Are there school memories that are pleasant? What about fun times with childhood friends?

There is a place for sad stories to be told, but how and when you do that is strictly up to you. Before I decide to share an unpleasant or sad memory, I always question myself as to why I want to write about that particular event and ponder it carefully. If the purpose of writing my memories is to help my family understand who I am today, then they need to know some of the hard times I have been through and the lessons I've learned by going through those hard times.

In the following Memory Example, I describe what our family experienced when the polio epidemic hit our small town. This memory explains many things to my children and grandchildren, including the trauma polio was to our family and the life-long effects of the disease. It should also give my family an understanding of some of the physical limitations they have seen in me over the years.

Along these same "sad" lines, I will eventually be writing about the children I have lost and the impact those losses had on my life – then and now. My children deserve to know about the siblings they never knew and my grandchildren need to know about the uncle and aunt they never met. When deciding to write about the "sad" things, there is a fine line between sharing and guarding your heart. Only you can determine about what you are comfortable writing.

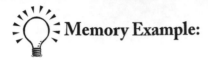 **Memory Example:**

Polio Strikes

I was nine years old, Philip was eight. It was the year 1951. A polio epidemic was spreading across the United States like wild fire. There was no vaccine and no way of stopping it. Many times, victims of the dreaded disease wound up crippled for life – usually in the legs and feet but it could affect any muscle in the body, including upper torso. Death was also a possibility. Up until now, no one in Boone had contracted polio.

One morning Philip and I both awoke with raging fever. We were VERY ill. In fact so ill that Mother and Daddy called Dr. Thomas in Fowler, CO (17 miles east of Boone) to come to our home. We were too sick to make the trip to his office. It is the only time I remember him coming to our home. By that time physicians were getting away from home visits and you were expected to go to their office. Dr. Thomas came, administered antibiotic shots (I'm assuming penicillin – but I'm not sure) and gave us cough medicine since we were both coughing non-stop. He diagnosed it as some kind of a virus, predicted that it would run its course and we would both recover. I don't ever remember having our blood tested in those days – not even when we were at his office. The doctors just went with their "gut feelings" and what they had learned in medical school.

Several days later, on a Saturday, after we seemingly had recovered, Philip developed a significant limp. Knowing that he had not injured himself, Mother quickly became concerned and headed for Dr. Thomas' office with him. The news was terrifying. Dr. Thomas immediately diagnosed it as polio and sent them right to the hospital in Pueblo. They stopped in Boone (which was between Fowler and Pueblo) to pick up Daddy, cover some details – I was supposed to have a piano recital that night (which my sister and her fiancé took me to) – and quickly went to Parkview Hospital. What a traumatic day for our family! The uncertainty of what it all meant hit like a 1000 lb. weight. Once they got to the hospital, Philip was immediately shut into a room (they called it an Isolation Room) completely alone. No one except the hospital staff was allowed in that room that day. It had a large window where you could stand in the hall and see him, but you were not allowed in there. Mother and Daddy were absolutely devastated. This was their baby and they were not allowed to touch, console or just be with him. One thing I remember Mother saying is that as she left him that night, (you were never allowed to stay all night at the hospital back then – in fact you had to leave by 8 p.m. – no exceptions) she could hear him crying over and over as she walked down the hall, "please, don't leave me" – it was right out of a horror movie.

The next morning Mother was at the hospital as soon as "visiting hours" opened. Daddy had several responsibilities at church - turning on the heat for the day, leading "Opening Exercises" before they broke into Sunday School classes (one of which he taught) and directing the choir. Since he could not be in the room at the hospital and since it was late on Saturday night when they got home with no way of finding replacements for all of his duties, he decided to go ahead with his Sunday responsibilities. We only had one car so Mother planned to come home in the afternoon and then they would go back together that evening - visiting hours were from 7-8 pm. I went with Daddy to church - I don't remember Susan and Rachel being there but they may have been.

There was a pot luck meal planned at the church that particular Sunday so Daddy and I stayed. I will never understand why Rev. Normand did this knowing what torment Daddy was feeling, but he asked Daddy to say the blessing over that meal. Right in the middle of his prayer, Daddy began to weep. I was standing right next to him, his broad shoulders were shaking and it took several seconds for him to gain enough composure to finish the prayer. Why the preacher did not step in and finish I don't know except times were tough back then and people stood on their own two feet with very little compassion shown by others. Rev. Normand had a little daughter named Kathy and she was a holy terror. Very little discipline ever went her way – in fact Philip and I just tolerated her when they came to our home – which was often – because they lived right across the street. She was spoiled to the core. Anyway, whenever I think of that particular event, Kathy Normand always surfaces in my memory because just as Daddy finished the blessing, she said in a very loud voice – for all to hear – "you are a baby" to Daddy. If I could have gotten my hands on her I probably would have done her bodily harm!! It was something I never forgot and I liked her even less from that day forward.

Because the prognosis was that Philip would be in the hospital for several weeks, the ladies of the church decided to fix a Sunshine Box for him. They wrapped the box with yellow paper and filled it with all kinds of wrapped gifts. The point of the Sunshine Box was that he would open one gift every day. This not only gave him things to entertain himself with (there were no televisions in the hospital rooms at that time and certainly no video games), but something to look forward to every day. There were books, coloring books, puzzles and crayons; anything that he could amuse himself with while he laid in that bed day after day.

I only remember going to see him once, and by that time I was allowed into the room. Actually, I don't think they made Mother and Daddy stay out of the room very long. I think they gave them some kind of sterile hospital gowns to wear and let them go in and be with him. Philip and I were very close and it broke my heart not to get to see him; so, after much begging, Mother and Daddy finally took me with them for that one visit. Philip says what he remembers about that visit was that when we got ready to leave I crawled up on the bed and kissed him on the forehead.

Once he came home we settled into a new routine. I remember him lying on the kitchen table on hot towels with Mother moving his legs back and forth, over and over to keep them from getting stiff. That was the therapy of the day. Every evening after that she fixed us bacon and tomato sandwiches, we split an eight ounce bottle (the bottle was glass) of Pepsi, she read us a story and then off to bed we'd go – just so happy to be back together we never gave her any grief about going to bed.

Philip got a lot of attention (and rightfully so) from this event. I've never quite understood why I never felt any jealousy over all of that attention and all of those gifts. The only thing I can figure out is that Mother, Daddy, Susan and Rachel must have made it a point to make me feel special and loved during that time because the love I had for him and the closeness we felt never wavered. The idea of what he must have been thinking in that hospital bed day after day still saddens my heart. I have praised God more than once over the years for healing him to the point of being able to lead a normal life with no visible crippling effects.

Over the years, I have had several doctors tell me that the main reason I have so much trouble with my neck and shoulders is because that is where the polio settled in my body. It wasn't something visible, like limping, so I never was treated. When I started dating and the boys tried to help me with my coat or jacket, it was very painful to reach around and stick my arms into the sleeves. It took years for me to realize that was a result of the polio. At the time I just thought "those dumb boys don't even know how to help me with my coat."

 Food for Thought:

1. Year the epidemic hit this family and their town
2. The polio disease is described
3. Distance to the doctor is explained, as well as the doctor's techniques

4. Hospital isolation is described

5. Trauma the family experienced as a result of the disease

6. Insensitivity of the pastor and his daughter

7. Commitment of Daddy to his church responsibilities

8. Love of the family for Philip

9. Discovery of writer's polio symptoms later in life

 Memory Triggers:

- **Traditions** - certain foods at holidays or certain songs sung at holidays? What about other times of the year? Mother's Day or Father's Day?

- **Tragedies** - in your family, friends and town

- **Vacations** - did your family go anywhere? Describe the trips - where, when, mode of travel, what did you do along the way, what did you see?

- **Values** - What were you taught about honesty, purity, loyalty, mercy or integrity? What was the work ethic in your family? What were you taught about good manners or being polite? What were you taught to do when you addressed an adult or they addressed you? Was the word "Ma'am or Sir" ever in your vocabulary?

Notes:

"Is This Therapeutic?"

While I am not a psychologist, I work with several pastoral counselors and, at different times, have had licensed therapists say this process is therapeutic. And one thing I know for sure is that it brings me great joy when I finish a story. While I am writing the story, I've found everything else going on in my life is turned off for that particular hour. An unexpected benefit of the memory writing process is that, once the story is complete and I pick up where I left off before I started writing, my mind seems to be refreshed and ready to tackle the rest of the day. May I suggest that using a part of our brain that has been unused (or even stagnate) for years stimulates our minds? I believe it does. The process of recording your stories seems to unlock a part of the memory that may have been perceived as "gone for good." The satisfaction of "completing a project" is a pleasant experience. One church consultant/ counselor said to me, "I wish my Mom would do this. It would be so good for her and I would love to have her memories written down. I'm missing so much." That is probably an understatement.

 **Memory Example:**

Baby Vitamins

When I awoke and went into the living room on Christmas, 1953, there was a little doll buggy under the tree. Up to that point I had used any old box I could find to put my dolls in. I lined the boxes with rags to make my dolls as comfortable as possible. Now I had my own baby buggy. I was thrilled! It was made out of wicker, painted brown, had metal wheels, was about 2-1/2 feet long and it had a little bonnet that moved to keep the sun and other weather elements off of my doll's face. I felt like the most fortunate little girl in town. Some of my friends had doll buggies and I had wanted one for a long time – at least it seemed like a long time to a 10 year old. In May of that same year (for my 10th birthday) I had been given my Horsman doll and she fit perfectly in my buggy.

I just about wore the wheels off that little buggy. There were no sidewalks or paved streets in town and the rough, dirt streets were very hard on it. I kept it shiny clean and pushed it up and down the street... especially if I was going to my friend Peggy's house to play. Peggy just lived down the street a few houses. She was the same age as me and I considered her to be my very best friend.

One day Peggy asked me to come to her house to play with our dolls. After getting permission from Mother to do just that, I put my doll into the buggy (she usually lay on my bed) and headed for Peggy's. Her bedroom was downstairs in the unfinished basement. She had several brothers and it seemed like Mrs. Strahn was never caught up on her laundry. There were piles and piles of clothes in that basement. To give the kids some privacy down there, Mr. Strahn had stretched a wire from one post to another and then hung blankets on the wire to make it look like their own rooms. Very primitive. No closet – just cardboard boxes for her folded clothes and nails in the walls to hang her clothes on. The one and only bathroom was upstairs. The basement was dark and dingy and always smelled musty to me but it was Peggy's room and I loved her so much I would have played in a ditch just to be with her.

Mr. Strahn was one of the few (what we considered) "Christian" men in our neighborhood. Their family attended church northeast of Boone and I thought they were very religious. Every evening they had devotions before everyone went to bed. Mr. Strahn read a few verses out of the Bible, then everyone was expected to pray before they finished their routine. Even when I spent the night – which was rare, because this made me so uncomfortable – I was expected to say some kind of prayer before we were allowed to go to bed. I did not like that. I was much too shy for that so I usually made some excuse to not spend the night. Their family eventually became the first missionary family I ever knew. They went to Barbados. I thought they had gone to the end of the earth and would be destroyed by either pirates or cannibals...

Back to my story about playing with Peggy. We didn't have baby bottles for our dolls and that seemed to be a very important item before we could actually get down to the business of playing house. We usually scrounged around for whatever we could find and, this particular day, Peggy found us each one empty baby vitamin bottle. She had a baby brother named Joseph at the time so I'm assuming that's where the vitamin bottles came from. They had a rubber top with an eye dropper on the end so it worked perfectly for our use. What we didn't do was rinse them out before playing with them. I knew the smell of those bottles was getting to me but I wanted to play so badly, I ignored the warning signs. By the time I got home, I was nearly sick – in fact, it was all I could do to get home before being sick. Mother had made a cake and *put black walnuts in the frosting for supper that evening. Well, somehow, the smell of that cake with the black walnuts, mixed with the smell of the vitamin bottles made an association with my being sick and to this day I cannot eat black walnuts. Nor did I buy that brand of vitamins when I started having children of my own!*

 Food for Thought:

1. Explanation of writer's aversion to black walnuts
2. Description of the Christmas gift
3. Description of the streets in town
4. Explanation of the friend's family's nightly devotions and the writer's fear of praying in public
5. Missionary family
6. Harsh living conditions in the friend's home

 Memory Triggers:

- **Visiting friends and relatives** – Did you have friends over for the afternoon? What did you do? Did relatives vacation with you in your home? Where did they sleep and what did you do? Did anyone ever come to stay for a lengthy amount of time? If so, describe the circumstances of their stay.

- **Weather** – were you ever caught in a snow storm or blizzard, sand storm, hurricane, cyclone or tornado? Where were you? How old were you? What happened? Did it do damage to your property? Were you or anyone you knew injured during the storm? Were you properly prepared and dressed for the storm? If not, why not?

Notes: _____

_____

_____

_____

_____

_____

"Can I Start With Current Events?"

I know of people who write their recent memories while everything is fresh in their minds. Recent events will often trigger older events, so add those triggers to your memory list for a future story. Many elderly people seem to have trouble remembering what they did in their 50s, 60s and 70s. Some people can remember their childhood but have a difficult time recalling what happened yesterday, last week, last month, or last year. If that is happening to you, don't despair, just start with what you can remember. Anything you write (even if it happened today or yesterday), will be history at some point and needs to be recorded.

 **Memory Example:**

The Train

I believe this event happened when I was in the 3rd or 4th grade.

One of the drawbacks to the location of our home was that we lived on the north side of the railroad tracks while all the town activities were on the south side of the tracks. There were four sets of tracks. It was a major thoroughfare for both the Santa Fe and the Missouri Pacific railroads. They sometimes barreled through town without stopping. During bean and wheat harvest time, they stopped and loaded the train cars with beans or wheat – sometimes blocking the crossing for what seemed like an endless length of time.

There was a train station in Boone. The person in charge of the train station usually lived in Boone – although their longevity never seemed more than a couple of years. There was a group of houses right along the tracks where some of the families of the men who worked for the railroad companies lived. These were usually very poor families. The houses were very small and actually shook when the trains came rolling and roaring through town, day or night.

In the early 1950s it was not uncommon for people (usually men) who were unemployed to hop into one of the railroad cars on a train, illegally, to go to another town to look for work or just for adventure. We called them "hobos" or "bums." Sometimes those men hopped off in Boone and went from one home to another begging for food. Mother never invited them in and she instructed us never to let them in, but on more than one occasion she gave them food. They sat on the front step, ate and left.

I don't remember walking with either Susan or Rachel to school when we were very young but we must have because it was fairly dangerous to cross those tracks. I hated crossing them, especially when I got big enough to do it alone.

In my younger years, there was no crossing guard nor were there blinking lights to let you know a train was coming – that came later after several people were killed crossing those tracks – either while they were walking or driving across them.

On this particular day, I was walking home from school by myself. I'm not sure where Philip was, because we usually had to walk home together. I wasn't necessarily afraid to cross the tracks by myself because, if you paid attention, you could hear the trains coming from far away. We had been trained to look both ways, even when we didn't hear anything before we crossed. I crossed the first two sets of tracks. Then there was some space, maybe 20 or 30 feet wide, before you came to the next set. As I got close to the next set, I could hear a train coming. It was about a mile away. The only reason for knowing that distance is because there is a large curve in the tracks about one mile west of town and the train was right at that curve. I wasn't quite to the tracks when I saw the train and I thought I had plenty of time to cross. I remember just kind of dawdling across the tracks. The trains always blew their whistle as they approached the crossing so when I heard the whistle I still didn't realize I was in any danger. Well, I can't imagine what I must have been thinking about because I wasn't more than six feet on the other side of those tracks when that train came whizzing by with its whistle blaring. Well, now I WAS scared! I think I ran all the way home hoping no one saw what a dumb thing I had just pulled.

I didn't mention it to anyone but the next day there was an "all school assembly." It was always a BIG deal when you had an all twelve grade assembly. The police and firemen from Pueblo County were there. I will never forget it. The policeman stood up on the stage and said, "yesterday afternoon, there was a very close call at the railroad tracks. One of the students in this room was almost hit by a train." I WAS HORRIFIED!!! I was scared to death he was going to single me out in front of the entire school and let everyone know how stupid I had been!

That may have been my first experience with the word "grace." No one ever mentioned my name – I've always wondered why. All they did was review all the safety precautions and rules of crossing those tracks.

Mrs. Atkins lived in a house fairly close to the train station and the tracks and I've always assumed she saw my stupid stunt and either called the school principal or the fire department and police. At any rate, whoever saw the incident (I suppose it might have been the train engineer – he had to be mortified) decided it was time to reaffirm the dangers of those tracks to the entire school on my behalf without ever saying a word to me.

From that day forward I had great respect for those trains and not only looked once but twice before ever stepping foot on a railroad track.

 Food for Thought:

1. Facts about what railroads ran through town
2. What crops were loaded onto the trains at that town
3. The writer was expected to cross the train tracks to and from school at an early age
4. Description of "hobos" and their use of trains for travel
5. Explanation of living conditions for people working for the train companies
6. Relief and wonder that the writer never had to admit to her careless actions

 Memory Triggers:

- **Wedding** – describe everything leading up to your wedding, talk about the ceremony itself. What did you wear? How many attendants did you have? Did it take place in a church, garden, home or justice of the peace? Did you have a reception? If so, write about that. Did you have a honeymoon? Where did you go? If the weather was a factor, write about it. What about the first wedding you ever attended or took part in? Did anything unexpected happen in any ceremony you were involved in or attended?

- **Your spiritual journey** – when were you first aware there was a God? Did you go to church? Where? How often? What did the church look like? When and where were you baptized? When and where did you learn to pray?

Notes:

"How Do I Make My Stories Interesting?"

When you are telling a story, you don't just give the facts; you try to make it interesting so people will listen. The same thing applies when you are writing your memories. Write descriptively. Along with the facts of who, what, where, when, why and how, you need to "set up" the story. If it is a story about being outside, describe the weather and what you were wearing. Was the sky blue? If so, how blue? Was it brilliantly blue, the color of the sea, or was it cloudy – or even black (perhaps a storm was brewing)? Did it smell of impending rain? After a storm, do you like the smell of wet dirt or the fresh, clean air? Does that smell trigger more memories? Was it a bright, sunny day with the promise of spring in the air? Was it a cold, brisk day in the middle of winter? Describe the sweet smell of the flowers or fields. Were you in a panic as you ran down the street to get help or were you on a morning stroll? How were you dressed? If you were a little girl, were you allowed to wear pants to protect your legs from the snow or sandstorms?

If you are describing the field of battle in a war, use words that will help transition the reader to that place. Were you in a jungle or desert? Were you crawling through cold mud? Was the temperature so hot you could barely breathe? Were you on some kind of ship (describe the ship) when the cyclone hit? How high were the waves? Did they roll over the bow of the ship? Did you stay in your bunk or did you have to be out on deck? Was there any damage to the ship? How long did the storm last? What was the color of the sea during the cyclone?

Describe the living conditions related to the story. Did you have dirt, linoleum, carpet or wood floors in your house? Did you have running water, a refrigerator or cook stove? What kind of heat did you have in your home? What did you wear to bed to keep warm in the winter? Did you have a cap on your head, socks or leggings? Did you ever put a hot rock or brick at the foot of your bed to keep your feet warm? Describe your bedroom. Did you have your own room or did you share a room with some of your siblings? Was the dirt in your yard as hard as cement or was it deep, rich and pliable – the kind in which you could grow anything you planted?

Did your family have an orchard? If so, what kinds of trees were in that orchard? Or if you were raised on a farm, what kind of crops did you raise? Was it an irrigated farm or dry land farm that depended upon the annual rain fall? What did you do with the harvest? Did you sell it to a Co-Op? Did your mother "can" some of the fruit or vegetables from the trees or from the garden? If you lived in the city, did your mother buy her produce from a vegetable/fruit stand? Did she bake bread? Did she pack your lunch for school? If so, what was usually in the lunch - peanut butter and jelly, bologna or eggplant sandwich? Were there special meals that she prepared that make your mouth water to this day? Have you ever tried to duplicate those meals? Were you successful or was it a complete flop? If it was a flop, what happened - did you burn the meal, was it undercooked, or did you leave an ingredient out?

Was your dad a "handyman"? Could he fix your car or do repairs around the house? If so, what kind of repairs? Was there a time when his "repairs" didn't quite work and there was a flood in the kitchen or the car was worse than before he started?

Did your mother work outside the home? If so, what did she do and how did she handle all of her "domestic duties/chores" and still manage to keep up with your school activities, etc.? Did she make your clothes? If so, where did she get the material or patterns to sew them?

How old were you in your story? Was anyone with you? Describe them. Were they glad to be there? Were they older or younger than you? Was it a planned event, something totally unplanned or an accident? Did you enjoy the event? Did anything funny happen during that event or does it make you smile just bringing it up from your "memory bank"? Did it change the way you think about things? Did it have a lasting impact on your life? Did you learn a life lesson from the event? For instance, "never put your hand on a hot stove" - that is simplified but it should help you get the idea.

What is the "moral of the story"? Not every story will have a "moral" but most of them will have some kind of conclusion. For example, if something happened that made you dislike a certain food, that would be a conclusion - from that point on, you didn't like that kind of food.

The point of this chapter is to help you think past the "facts" with questions to help bring out the details that can be woven into your story. What will keep your family on the edge of their seats and intrigued as to how the story will end? Include lots of description and your family will be more than willing and ready to read your next story.

 **Memory Example:**

Frosty the Snowman

My fourth grade year seems to retain more memories than any of my other elementary classes. The teacher's name was Mrs. Beckett. She lived in a tiny, two room hut just across the alley from the school grounds. There were three or four of these huts – none of them with modern conveniences – and that's where the teachers who did not have families stayed. I don't think they were paid very much to work in the Boone School District and they could not afford to drive from Pueblo, so they put up with these horrible little places to live during the school year.

Mrs. Beckett looked just exactly like someone you often see in movies depicting a buxom "old maid" school teacher. Her hair was red, she was on the "chunky" side, her voice was raspy and she did not allow any nonsense in her class. I learned my multiplication tables in her class – that seemed to be her mission – making sure we knew how to multiply before we got to the fifth grade class where we learned how to divide. She drilled us over and over several times a day – sometimes making it fun with games, the other times she just held up a card and we were expected to know the answer at any given minute. She kept her lunch money (\$.25 a day) inside the neckline of her blouse and we students thought that was very odd – if not funny.

She must have thought we were still young enough to get tired because every day when we came in from the lunch recess, she made us put our heads on our desk and rest while she sang "Froggie Went A Courtin" – every verse. Her voice was very deep and husky but I actually began to look forward to her solo every day. I remember ducking my head down in my arms on my desk and smiling as she sang.

When we got to the fourth grade we were old enough to have "music class." Mrs. Beckett did not teach music. I think the music teacher was Mrs. DeWall (who also taught 3rd grade). Mrs. DeWall must have thought this particular music class had some talent because about the time the weather began to turn cold, she decided we should put together a production of Frosty the Snowman and present it to the elementary classes. I was the mother of the children building Frosty. The principal

91

of the school liked the program so much, he arranged for us to travel to the little elementary school in South Avondale (five miles west and two miles south of Boone) to present it there.

I had a solo singing part. I stood next to the piano and sang while the children built Frosty. There was a little Spanish girl sitting in the front row of the audience and she leaned over to the little girl sitting next to her and said, "isn't she pretty?" Well, I nearly lost it. I had NEVER been told I was "pretty" before. Mother and Daddy (and I suspect many other parents of that era) thought that if you made over your children or told them they were pretty or handsome, it would spoil them and they would grow up worthless, so as far as I know, I never heard those words from my family. When that little girl said that, I felt like I was floating on air the rest of the day. Someone actually thought I was pretty. WOW! She watched me all through the performance and I eventually learned her name, although it escapes me at this writing. She and I became friends once we got into Jr. High at Excelsior Jr. High School but that is another story for another time. Our little production went off without a "hitch" and we were asked to do it one more time – this time for the entire student body of Boone School.

 Food for Thought:

1. Teacher's name and attributes
2. Teaching goals and methods for 4th grade
3. Living conditions for teachers
4. Music production brought into the classroom
5. "Going on the road" with the class's first musical production
6. Impact of a compliment on the writer

 Memory Triggers:

- **Your town** – describe what the main street looked like – was it paved? Did it have street lights? What businesses were located on the main street? What was the population and altitude of the town you grew up in (approximately, this does not have to be exact)? Was your town incorporated? Did it have a sheriff or police department? Are there stories relating to either of these? What about a town judge or constable?

- **Writing** - poetry, stories, letters, articles? Who taught you to write – parent, teacher, sibling?

Notes: _____

S o now it is up to you. I trust after reading this book you are excited about writing your stories for your family and I believe you will find it very enjoyable. I'd like to leave you with two short stories...

I've been encouraging a friend of mine, for several years, to start writing for her family. She was raised with several siblings, many of whom have passed away. They grew up in one of the "southern" states in the U.S. in the 1930s so you can imagine the history and stories stored up in that family. She has ignored my pleas, concentrating on her artistic talent (I own several of her paintings) and her family. She presently lives in a different state several hundred miles from me but we frequently stay in touch. To my complete surprise and delight, when I checked my voicemail a few weeks ago, her familiar voice said "Lana, why didn't you tell me writing my memories would be so enjoyable!" Then she proceeded to tell me that she had jotted down several memories on a 2"x3" note pad and she enjoyed it so much she was graduating to a full-sized tablet. She continues to write, and is now encouraging others to do the same thing!

The other incident also came from a voicemail. Several years ago, my brother and sister-in-law lived with my husband and me the year I began to write my first book of memories for my children and grandchildren. During the seven months they were in our home and for the three following years, when I approached the subject that my sister-in-law should do this for her family (she grew up in the Midwest – with a completely different set of circumstances than the friend I just described), her comments were always "Lana, I can't remember like you do...I don't have enough to share." I asked her if she would read the book you currently hold in your hands, to which she reluctantly agreed. I think if the truth was known, she read it out of her love for me and to get me to stop nagging her, not because she had any interest in writing her stories. One evening when arriving home from work, there was a voicemail from her that I have not been able to bring myself to delete to this day. It says "Lana, you are absolutely right. After reading your book and looking at the memory triggers, the memories began to storm back and I can't wait to get started writing."

I hope you feel the same. It has been my pleasure to put this "how to" book together for you. If you use the encouragement, theories and triggers included here, you and your family are in for a very rewarding and satisfying experience. History is being rewritten every day by people who didn't live it, because people have not been willing to tell their stories. Don't let that happen to your family - share your stories and leave them the legacy and blessing of really knowing "why" you do "what" you do and "who" you have become. Your family will appreciate your efforts and your memories will be cherished for years.